Invitation to Sout...

Invitation
to
South Africa

Gerald Sparrow

LONDON
NEVILLE SPEARMAN

First published in Great Britain in 1974
by Neville Spearman Limited
112 Whitfield Street, London W1P 6DP

SBN 85435 342 9

Typeset in 12/13pt Aldine by
Specialised Offset Services Limited, Liverpool
and printed by The Compton Press Ltd.,
Compton Chamberlayne, Salisbury, Wilts.
Bound by W. & J. Rawlinson Ltd., London

Contents

1.	Author to reader	7
2.	Modern South Africa	11
3.	Towards the Cape	21
4.	Cape Town and the Cape	29
5.	A Stopover at Kimberley	36
6.	"Joburg"	46
7.	Durban and Natal	53
8.	The Great Game Reserves	61
9.	Some special resorts	70
10.	The Summing-up	86
	Appendix	92

1

Author to reader

The urge to take a holiday is as old as nomadic man, as new as the jet age. What everyone is looking for is somewhere different. There is nothing wrong with home, but it is a great place to come back to. After being anchored for so long, the ship must sail away. The man, the woman and the children must pack and go on a voyage of discovery, or in simpler terms, have a holiday. Change is the most essential ingredient in a holiday. As Sir Winston Churchill pointed out to his overworked staff: 'All you need is a change. We're going to Washington next week.'

South Africa represents to Europeans and Americans the greatest possible change. It is a country with many races, with several climates, with a great choice of food and wine, with abundant wild life, with some of the best entertainment in the world, a country with space and great contrasts where today is more important than yesterday and tomorrow more important than today, a rich country with a limitless future where the hotels are superb, the roads excellent – a motorist's paradise – and where the people welcome the visitor openly and generously.

In a world where turmoil, strife and violence are becoming alarmingly common, South Africa has peace, law and order. These are some of the reasons why the sophisticated tourist is seeking out South Africa, ready perhaps to take a longer holiday in order to see the whole country, the magnificence of Johanesburg, the charm of Cape Town and the unique appeal of Durban, where the great rollers of the Indian Ocean crash on to miles of uncrowded beach. And this holiday must include the wild life of South Africa at Kruger National Park, a vast territory, or more intimately at such game reserves at Malamala, perhaps the most comfortable of all the game park lodgings, where one goes out to see the lions, the antelope and the giraffe, the buffalo and the rhino in an open Land Rover, as exciting an experience as any tourist can ask for.

Yes, South Africa is the place which one must visit or miss an unforgettable experience. It is worth the journey, now so fast and so luxurious. Before I paid my first visit to the country I expected South Africa to take its place in the storehouse of my memory along with the other countries I had visited in Europe, the Near and Far East, Egypt and all North Africa, and North America including Canada and the United States. South Africa did not conform. It was not just another memory. For me it was a unique experience which I shall never forget. Having led a life with much adventure and great changes I was not expecting anything so different, so exciting, and so satisfying. No-one could be bored on a visit to South Africa. The pace and vast extent of the South African scene make that impossible. It is a country which appeals to everyone, all ages and all nationalities. If English is the greatest tourist language then this helps, too, for English is spoken by a great number of South Africans in the cities, the towns, and in the countryside. One feels at home in

South Africa and yet one's visit is a constant adventure seeing a life one had not dreamt of, meeting a people so confident and extrovert, tasting the flavour of a country in which tomorrow is married to yesterday.

This is the general picture and because I have so recently experienced it I would like you to realise that it is unique. It is the one holiday you will never regret. But let me mention in more detail what the possibilities, the amenities, and the lure of South Africa consist of. Why is South Africa in a class by itself as a tourist's mecca? Every visitor will have a different answer to this question, so let us consider first what most tourists are seeking and then see how South Africa meets these demands.

The tourist of course includes the visiting business man and his requirements may be specialised. He is often doing his work in the large cities and relies on transport, the telephone, comfortable and reliable hotels, easy communications by air inter-city and recreation often in the evening which may be the only time he has free. All these requirements are met throughout the Republic. And, should he have time for sport, as we shall see, South Africa is a premier sporting country.

Many tourists, perhaps the majority, will not be coming on business but to have the holiday of their lives. With time to spare they want to see everything but, at the same time, they want to have time to relax. These tourists often decide to travel by air and if they choose South African Airways they will be in South Africa from the moment of their take-off. In the giant jumbo jets, which are luxurious in the exact meaning of the word, they will enjoy what I regard as the best flight in the world for comfort, for service, for reliability and for cuisine. On waking the next morning, there is the great scarlet sun of Africa climbing into the heaven on the plane's port side. There is no sight quite like it. It is African, magnificent, and inspiring.

The tourists may be travelling to stay with friends or they may have booked in at an hotel in one of the cities. Whatever their itinerary it will contain a diversity of country, climate — variations of good climate — wonderful motor ways, opportunity for every kind of sport — sailing, aqua sports, golf, tennis, and the supreme show of South Africa, the Game Reserves.

Game reserves, in a European context, give no idea of the extent or grandeur of the 'Game Parks' of South Africa. These are in fact great stretches of territory, as big as small European states, containing all the wild animals in their natural setting. They have not been imported. They have always been there. And it is encouraging to know that the advanced policies of the Government in the promotion and care of these great sanctuaries has resulted in certain animals that seemed to be heading for extinction being saved and becoming multiplied. The white rhino is a good example of this. Now hundreds of these animals roam their natural habitat. We will discuss this feature of South African life and tourism in the chapter devoted to it. But, to sum up, there is no field of activity that the tourist may need that is not available. For instance all the major towns have good libraries, and the South African Press, a uniquely independent variety of newspapers and magazines, marshalls the world news as well as the domestic scene.

I have set out the promise and in the chapters that follow I will suggest how the reality meets that promise. But, before we look into this, I will devote a chapter to the country itself, for no intelligent tourist would wish not to know in broad outline the background of the country he has chosen to visit. I have called this chapter 'Modern South Africa' and I hope it will make the subsequent, detailed chapters more entertaining and informative.

2

Modern South Africa

Before your plane touches down at Jan Smuts airport, or your ship drops anchor in a South African harbour, it adds greatly to the interest of a holiday if you know the size and shape and something of the way of life of the unique country you are visiting. As to the details of accommodation, planned tours and the immense variety of sightseeing available, the South African Tourist Corporation (a list of its offices appears in the appendix of this book) will render you comprehensive assistance, but in order to appreciate the kind of country that is modern South Africa you have either to read one of the excellent books on the Republic now in print, or, if you are less ambitious, the kind of resumé of the country's characteristics that this chapter will give you may be enough for your purposes and may even induce you to explore further into the remarkable story of this great nation.

The basic facts that you need to know about South Africa in order to appreciate the background for your visit can be summarised in this way:

1. South Africa is a big country, almost half a million square miles in extent and much of it is at an altitude of from four to six thousand feet. Although the climate is temperate, the summer heat is abated by the height of much of the country and the air, pollution free, will help to make you or keep you fit. As the country is of course south of the equator, the seasons are the opposite to those enjoyed by Europeans and Americans. Their winter is our summer and their summer is our winter. Opinions vary as to the best season for a visit, because all seasons can be enjoyed, but personally I found the late autumn and spring lovely in South Africa, although if you live in Europe the temptation to escape the winter may be irresistible.

2. Although the climate of Johannesburg and Pretoria, the capital, differs from that of Durban, which is much more humid and less bracing, and Durban differs from the Cape which is clement and without great variations, and indeed a really lovely climate, all over South Africa you get an immense amount of sunshine. This accounts for the deep tans of South Africans. They are accustomed to the sun and their passion for sport — as well as work — takes them out of doors much more than is common in Europe. Cape Town has about twice the number of hours of sunshine that London enjoys, almost three thousand hours annually. This means that the sun for your holiday is 'guaranteed' and the comparison holds even as between South Africa and the South of France. South Africa has about fifty per cent more sunshine than, say Cannes or Monte Carlo. This one factor alone really makes a South African holiday. To get up in the morning knowing that the sun will greet you, and to be sure that your plans, whatever they may be, will not be ruined by the weather, this gives a holiday a dimension and a certainty that few other countries can match. Rainfall is fairly spread and a

thunderstorm can be an epic experience. I only experienced one, motoring on a road returning to Johannesburg. Like so many things in South Africa it seemed larger than life. There is no 'monsoon' type rain that plagues countries such as India. Rain is not a weather problem in South Africa. Always the sun rides high in the heavens.

3. South Africa is a multi-racial nation, the largest single group being the white South Africans who are made up of men and women of Dutch, English, German, French and, to a lesser extent, immigrants from other European countries. There are two main languages, Afrikaans and English. Language presents no difficulties to the majority of tourists in South Africa so a lot of frustration and even worry is eliminated.

The Bantu races who total over 15 million (15,057,559 in the 1970 census) are divided into tribes or races that are quite distinct and sometimes not entirely compatible. The Zulus number just over four million, the Xhosa, four million, the Tswana and the North and South Sotho tribes each number over a million and there are five other main racial groups. These groups are as distinct as European national groups. It is a common misunderstanding to think that all the black citizens of South Africa are one large body. However, white and black have equal citizenship, equal protection under the law and equal access to the Courts which are acknowledged to be independent and of the highest standard. In planning the future of their country the South Africans have decided on a policy of separation instead of the integration common in Europe and in Portuguese African territories. Out of this concept arises the new Bantustans which are African states due to become fully independent, the most advanced being the Transkei, a lovely fertile land bordering the Indian ocean.

4. South Africa has great wealth both at the present time and potentially. For instance its coal resources are enough for five hundred years. Its gold and diamonds are world famous and copper, platinum and manganese are produced on a very large scale. The intense industrialisation including many other industries such as agriculture and wine production ensures that the visitor and especially the visiting businessman will obtain all the ancillary business services he requires. The Banks and Insurance Companies in particular are run on the most modern lines and provide a great diversity of services. Britain is the largest customer for South African goods but many other nations, including Japan and the United States have a large trade with the Republic.

For foreign companies wishing to establish themselves in South Africa the way is made as easy as possible. Broadly speaking, South Africa welcomes everyone, communists and atheists excluded. Labour is plentiful in many areas but the supply does not always meet the demand. This accounts for the large number of Africans from the independent African states to the North who seek work permits in South Africa because of the better wages obtainable and the better housing and living conditions and, perhaps equally important, the complete protection from molestation or any form of interference which police in South Africa ensure. African wages have risen sharply in recent years to keep pace with the rise in the cost of living but are still modest as compared with European and of course American standards. The equable and reasonable tax system acts as an attraction to foreign investment and the establishment of offices or branch offices in the Republic.

5. The word 'apartheid' is much used in the western press to describe the separation of the races in South Africa. The

14

visitor may not even notice it. Its chief characteristic is that the Europeans, the Bantu, the 'coloureds' and the Indians have their own part of the city or town to themselves instead of being mixed residentially. Politics do not concern the visiting tourist as a rule but he needs to know that this system exists. It has ensured peace and security for nearly seventy years for Africans and Europeans alike.

6. The Government of South Africa has a federal base arising out of its history and pursuing this division of administrative power, the chief executive offices are situated in Pretoria, the administrative capital, the Law Courts are located in Bloemfontein, while the Assembly sits in Cape Town. The National Party has formed the Government for many years as its form of progressive conservatism appeals to a wide spectrum of white South African opinion, but there is a substantial opposition United Party and a very small Progressive Party. When the Bantustans reach Statehood there will of course be fully empowered independent African legislatures. Visiting businessmen will find the Department of Commerce a valuable and well informed contact while the ordinary tourist needing information or help can rely on the Department of Tourism. There is also a progressive and efficient Department of Information.

7. The chief cities of South Africa are Johannesburg with a million and a half inhabitants, Cape Town with just over a million, Durban with over 700,000, Pretoria with over half a million, and such towns as Bloemfontein, Germiston and East London with smaller but substantial populations. All these figures rise annually and quite rapidly because it is a feature of the South African scene that the population, like its industry and wealth, is constantly waxing. The

visitor will notice this aspect of South African life from the day he or she arrives. The future is looked to with absolute confidence. South Africans do not doubt. They believe absolutely in the destiny and assured future progress of their country.

8. Entertainment in South Africa, which formerly relied to a large extent on visiting talent, is now advanced and sophisticated. The South African 'circuit', including of course Johannesburg, Durban and Cape Town, still attracts the top European artists on tour and music and the arts generally are well cared for especially in the largest cities. Opera, ballet and straight plays including comedy can be seen and enjoyed in any of the large cities. The cinema is omnipresent. However the cinema patron will not be embarrased by the type of pornographic film, usually miserable in quality, that have put off audiences in Europe and America. This reflects the strong influence of the Churches, the Dutch Reformed Church, the Anglican Church, and a number of lesser denominations including the Catholic Church. South Africans seek to maintain standards and they manage to do it without appearing prudish or limiting peoples enjoyment. For instance at the very fine hotels in Cape Town and Johannesburg (A list of major hotels appears in the appendix) there are first rate 'cabarets' and the atmosphere is relaxed and international.

9. Food and wine add immeasurably to the enjoyment of a South African holiday. The wine is now world famous but it still to this visitor tastes better in South Africa than after it has 'travelled.' Drunk in Europe it is still, in my opinion, better than many Spanish or Italian wines, but drunk in South Africa it is supreme. Each connoisseur will choose his own labels and vintages. Perhaps it is enough if I say that a cooled or chilled dry wine of the Chablis type

grown in South Africa and drunk fairly fresh is a delicious experience.

The cuisine is international, is good in the large hotels and tends to be excellent in restaurants. The sea food including crabs, prawns and lobsters is magnificent. There are also 'typically' South African dishes. Among these I indulged in: kebabs called sosaties, boerewors, a spiced sausage, bobotie a curried mince. Some of these dishes were clearly introduced into South Africa by the Malays, who form a special group within the Asian community and who have kept their own customs as well as their Moslem faith, in contrast to the Indian community who tend to be Hindu or Christian. The Bantu prepare maize in their own way that makes it look (and taste?) rather like Scotch porridge. They wash it down with the beer they brew themselves.

All races in South Africa and all visitors enjoy the extraordinary variety of fresh fruit. Returning to Cape Town by road I bought mangoes from roadside sellers for a price of about twentyfive cents for two dozen. They were delicious, ripe and sweet. Of course there is every kind of semi-tropical fruit, bananas, guava, pawpaw, melon and many others. A country with such wine and fruit is doubly blessed.

10. The tourist, if he reads the Western or American press may be surprised to find a very independent press operating in South Africa, often critical of the establishment. The top papers either in Afrikaans or English bear comparison with the best in Europe. Die Burger the premier newspaper in the Afrikaans language, occupies the kind of position that The Times in Britain once commanded before it became 'fashionable.' There is no dull conformity in South Africa. As one would expect from a populace largely of Dutch or English descent,

people hold their own views individually and strongly, but all are united by love of their country and a determination to see that it is not subverted. Patriotism is still an honoured tradition in South Africa and the young men do their military service in order to be prepared for the unlikely event of aggression by any other power or confederacy of powers.

The tourist will take back with him his own estimate of the country, his own assessment of the South African way of life, but two points will probably occur to him. Public affairs in South Africa, even that portion which covers the Bantustan projects and the future independence of the African States seems to be conducted with much less acrimony than in Europe or America. There is often much good will, and good manners on both sides. Another aspect of the overall situation is that any attempt by outsiders to interfere with the internal Government of South Africa would meet with instant and overwhelming resistance from all races in South Africa. The policy of separation does not mean that on the basic question of sovereign independence the country is divided. *Ex unitate vires* is the national motto — and it is the nation's resolve as well.

If you are already well acquainted with the outline of modern South Africa you will not have needed this resumé to inform you of the kind of country you are visiting, but if you have not visited South Africa before and have not read much on the subject, this very brief outline touching from necessity only on salient points, may help you to understand what you see, hear and read more fully. To complete the picture now that we have a sketch of the tree, we need to know the outstanding points of the story that went before.

The first people to call at the Cape were, as usual in the 15th century, the Portuguese. Then came the Dutch. Jan Van Riebeeck founded for the Dutch East India Company a Trading Station at Table Bay. The natives whom the earliest settlers encountered were Hottentots and Bushmen. A greatly reduced population of Bushmen aborigines still exists. The Hottentots tended to mix with the early European arrivals, accounting in part for the two million 'coloured' population today.

In 1688 French Huguenots, the victims of political persecution arrived and found a haven in South Africa. Their names are still prominent among South African families but they are of course entirely and for centuries have been assimilated with other European stock. The British arrived in 1820 and in powerful force and numbers. Britain at this time was the most aggressive imperial power, with the possible exception of Russia, and the British established themselves in the Cape. Much later from the mid 1830's onwards the Afrikaners who found British rule somewhat irksome tended to trek North to new country and they crossed eventually the Vaal river into what is now the Transvaal.

About the same time that all this was happening, the Bantu tribes and especially the Zulus, were seeping down the east coast moving through the rich grazing lands to the north of Durban. Durban was another English stronghold and while the Afrikaners established their independence in the Transvaal and in the Orange Free State, clashes started to occur between the oncoming Zulus and the expanding areas of the Afrikaners and the British. This lead to two 'Zulu wars' which would take a book to describe even in outline, so fascinating is the story.

The present independent Republic of South Africa, consisting of the four Provinces of the Cape of Good Hope, the Orange Free State, the Transvaal and Natal, was founded on the 31st of May 1961 after exactly fifty years as the Union of South Africa and a member of the Commonwealth. Before that, the unhappy event of the

19

'Boer' war had bedevilled the concord and peace of the nation. The present Prime Minister is Mr B.J. Vorster and his National Party have a large majority both in the Senate and in the House of Assembly.

This in barest outline is the story of South Africa that would take a very long book to tell in any detail, but perhaps from this brief summary of life as it is today and the events that went before, the reader who decides to visit South Africa will at least have in his mind some notion of the geography, climate, racial roots, vegetation, industry, political make-up, and way of life that will be the background of the South Africa of today. Later he will get to know at first hand. Whether his stay is long or short, whether he travels simply or de luxe, wherever he comes from he may be certain of one thing – a warm South African welcome. This is a confident and happy people and that confidence and happiness is infectious and communicates itself to those who come to explore this new young giant among the nations. It has so much to offer the enquiring traveller that his stay should be truly memorable.

3

Towards the Cape

The enjoyment of a South African holiday depends largely, as do all holidays, on not being in a hurry and, if possible, not having a schedule. If a schedule is your very life, it should be made so flexible that you can easily be diverted, for it is by being diverted that you will get to know the peculiar flavour of South Africa, its abundant and cosmopolitan life, its mountains wrapped in a characteristic blue haze, its infinite variety of life and leisure. If you can resist the temptation of wanting to see everything and having to reach a certain destination at a certain time, you will greatly increase the pleasure and diversity of your visit. Rest is one of the keys for a successful holiday combined with change, certainly for those already in middle age. For the young all things are possible.

Basically, assuming you touch down at Jan Smuts airport, you have to choose the method of your holiday. This, you will find, divides itself into at least three easy and pleasant choices. You can either fly by the magnificent network of internal domestic flights of South African

Airways to your chief destinations and foray from each as the spirit takes you. Alternatively, you can hire a self-drive car (keep to the left of the road) and motor yourself around South Africa stopping when or preferably before you are tired, taking advantage of the fine trunk roads that link up all the chief towns and cities. It is a motorists' paradise and a three mile stretch of clear road is not at all uncommon, or you can make a base in Durban or Cape Town or Johannesburg or some smaller centre and do your sightseeing by taking the extremely well organised bus tours that are arranged to the chief tourist attractions. It is largely a question of expense. The three methods of planning I have indicated are more or less in order of cost. That is to say flying around may cost you a little more while public organised transport is always cheapest.

I am going to assume that you intend to fly around the country, staying at three or four of the chief cities from which tourist tours radiate. However, in case you choose one of the other methods of seeing South Africa I have set out in an Appendix, as well as South African Airways internal flight schedules, the chief long distance bus tour operators, the firms who specialise in Game Park tours and some reliable car-hire operators as well.

You will decide if you want to stay over-night in Johannesburg, as I did, or go directly to your first base of exploration. I stayed the night only a short car ride from the airport because after a long flight at say 40,000 feet in even the most comfortable and indeed luxurious aircraft I think an immediate evening of complete relaxation is needed. You will choose your hotel. There are more than half a dozen hotels in the very top class. They are all graded by the Government on a star system and their prices vary accordingly. Nothing is cheap any more. What I did find was that in South Africa bills were correct and you get outstanding value for money. In the appendix which forms an important part of this book I have listed some of the major hotels.

So your first night would be spent in the quiet luxury of a great Johannesburg Hotel and you will almost certainly be able to dine in a dining room that gives you a panoramic view of the city lights. The city itself vibrates with life as you will see as you set out in the morning thoroughly refreshed, but tonight it is relaxation. There will be a first-rate menu carefully and skillfully cooked by a European chef and afterwards dancing and a cabaret. This will be your first taste of South African wine in South Africa and this in itself, if you are a wine man, will be a delight to you. Like so much else in this country the wines tend to be young, vigorous and enchanting. I will devote a chapter to food and wine but in fact you will discover much for yourself according to your tastes and mood.

Several times while touring in South Africa I was asked by fellow tourists how to treat the Bantu servants and waiters. The answer is obvious. Those who formerly experienced being waited on by Chinese boys in the East know that the key to success is a mixture of firmness and courtesy. The Bantu does not appreciate being asked. He expects to have a request if not an order, but if it is politely put he appreciates it as we all do. There is no problem here. In many of the major hotels the waiters will be South Africans who often have a strong sense of humour. They also take a pride in their work. The Hotel direction will invariably be white and you will travel by white transport. This is the custom of the country and you will find the enjoyment of your holiday greatly increased if you do not criticise the customs and way of life of South Africa. You will find when you get to know the real background that separation works and is a big factor in assuring that black and white live at peace with one another.

If you care to follow the route I took — and there are many alternatives open to you — after a leisurely breakfast you will motor to the airport and board an internal South African Airways jet for Durban. We are only going to stay a night in Durban at this stage. We will return to Durban and to Johannesburg later. The object of going to Durban is to start your trip in stages and after staying overnight to motor from Durban to Cape Town along a fine road that takes you through a variety of fascinating country.

The flight to Durban is quite short, a little under an hour, and here you are on the Indian Ocean in a warm somewhat humid climate but with a sea breeze that makes it exactly right for many visitors. It is not my habit in this book to suggest where you should stay, but on this your second night in South Africa I am going to break the rule and invite you to put up at the Edward Hotel which of course overlooks the ocean and is a grand, even regal hotel. The Edward is, for many, nostalgic, with its Prince of Wales feathers as a decoration motif and its very traditional staff who will attend to your requirements with swift smiling efficiency. The food, too, is excellent, especially the fish and shell fish dishes that literally come out of the ocean on to your plate. If you have children with you there is a wonderland of fun between the hotel and the sea which children find entrancing.

You will notice a large number of Indians here. They originally came from their own country to work in the sugar plantations but later, when other labour became more available, were offered generous terms to return to their own country. Hardly any accepted. And the leaders of the Indian community I met were quite certain that they only wished to stay in South Africa. The new aggressive India with a war against Portugal, a war against their sister nation Pakistan, and a long and terrifying colonial war against the Nagas was not the India which

they or their forbears had left and they were determined
not to return. Nor did any independent African country
attract them. They have now multiplied to an influential
community of over half a million – by far the largest
Indian community in Africa. They have been given some
fine sights to build their modern houses, and many of
them are now business and professional men of good
standing. Many of course are still in skilled or semi-skilled
jobs and you will see them, intelligent, quick and efficient,
in the Durban hotels. The comparative wealth and standing
of the Indian community is a tribute to their industry and
also a tribute to the toleration and good sense of the South
African Government who have converted a nucleus of farm
workers into one of the best organised and happiest
communities in Africa. Separation does not worry the
Indians. They have always declined to integrate, in any
case preferring to nurse their own religion, customs and
way of life. This has been held against them in independent Africa but in South Africa it fits into the general
pattern. South Africa is now their country and the days
when they arrived as contract workers and all thoughts of
repatriation are long past. It is remarkable that whereas in
some African States a fairly small Indian community is
found indigestible, in South Africa a very large and
prosperous community is found acceptable, adding to the
life and trade of the Republic.

If you love the Edward Hotel as I loved it you will be
loath to leave but, as I promised, we are returning here and
meantime you will at your leisure be inspecting your hire
car in which you are going to make this long trip of around
eight hundred miles. I hope you will take at least three
days in the process and staying overnight at East London,
and at Oudtshoorn. If you prefer a much shorter drive you
can hire your car in East London, making the short air trip
from Durban to East London by S.A.A plane. We will

25

describe East London in the chapter devoted to the South African towns of interest but meanwhile let us say something about the delights of your last step, Oudstshoorn. This is semi-desert ostrich country and those who have not seen a great ostrich farm have missed something worth seeing. Originally the ostrich feathers were in great demand for Edwardian ladies' hats but now the most diverse uses have been discovered for them, the feather being unique in strength, durability and softness. I arrived on an ostrich plucking day and it takes three men to control each bird. The bird is put into a stall where its ripe feathers are fairly painlessly taken out. Great care has to be exercised, for a blow from an ostrich's foot, struck downward after being raised, can cause very serious injury. If you must and you are a light weight you can ride an ostrich. It is not a diversion I recommend. But the Ostrich farms and the delightful old homes on quite a grand scale of the Ostrich Barons are well worth seeing. It is often hot in Oudtshoorn. You will need a big hat and your wife a sunshade. You will not regret the minor discomforts. There is no animal as strange and as useful as the ostrich. Every piece of the ostrich is eventually made use of. The life of those who farm this great bird is a special way of life and it requires a special kind of endurance and expertise to make a success of ostrich farming.

Of course it is worth staying the night in Oudtshoorn. There is a choice of decent hotels but I stayed at a Holiday Inn one of a chain of such places throughout the Republic. I was prejudiced against anything called a Holiday Inn that had a somewhat garish sign outside, but once installed I found the reception, the cuisine, the informal atmosphere, the bedroom and the grounds altogether pleasing. Holiday Inns are reasonable in their prices. They are extending rapidly throughout the land and seem to provide for a demand by South Africans as well as visitors. The ostriches will take up your first day and at least half a day you must spend at the Cango Caves. Again I have never been a great cave man, but this truly magnificent chain of caves in the mountain side is the newest wonder of the world, as great in its way as any that went before. Over millions of years the slow action of water has opened up these huge caverns and the water itself has frozen into grotesque and beautiful patterns. On the walls the prehistoric remains of great animals and past cultures are embedded in the rock — a stupendous sight.

Except for the very recently discovered caverns, the caves are open to the public, and the first two or three will be enough to show you the beauty and immense size of these underground temples to the past. In these the lighting is spectacular and guides, who know their job, show parties around. Some visitors have suggested that the introduction to the caves which the guides give should be less devoted to the Almighty and more to the scientific miracle. I disagree. I found the Caves awe-inspiring and an appropriate setting to refer to the work of God. That it has a scientific explanation we all know. As we are on the subject of minor criticism, perhaps it will not be taken amiss if I mention that the text of the guides' story should confine itself to relevant matters. Our guide had confused King Edward the seventh with his grandson King Edward the eighth. But we cannot all know these difficult details and the amenities of the Cango Caves including an excellent restaurant and even a changing room, are beyond reproach. Do not miss the Cango Caves. I guarantee you will be thrilled by an experience nowhere in the world to be seen on this scale. The Cango Caves are by far the greatest, the best preserved, and the most beautiful in the world today.

If you must hurry on along the lovely road that leads to Cape Town, our first destination, by all means do so but I suggest that you linger one night at Mossel Bay, a delightful resting place by the sea. Then make an early morning start and arrive in Cape Town in time for lunch, so that you have half a day of rest and a night of diversion and entertainment before you explore the charming city of Cape Town. Explore also the eastern and western Cape, making Cape Town your headquarters. This will take you at least a week and you will find yourself becoming increasingly addicted to the Cape way of life which is an easy one. The pressures are off here. A kind climate, a cultured people, prosperity, a long history and a growing tradition combine to make the Cape the super holiday resort for the European who comes from old countries, and those who come from North America find the quiet charm completely captivating once they have unwound and realised that the pace here is gentle, the delights to be savoured and that there is time to appreciate and enjoy it all. For this is one of the South African tourist centres that are world famous and the South Africans both through their Government and at a personal level delight in extending you a welcome. The Cape is a happy place.

4

Cape Town and the Cape

By the time you arrive in Cape Town you will have travelled through some of the most romantic countryside of South Africa. The flowers are more in evidence here and they are more exotic. Apart from the Protea, the national flower, which likes a sandy soil, as you approach Cape Town you will see houses with gardens that harbour frangipani, hibiscus and a great variety of semi-tropical flowers and plants including orchids. So you arrive and enter the centre of Cape Town. There is a wide choice of hotels for you to choose from, one in particular has fine well kept gardens, but perhaps, at any rate for the businessman, a centrally situated hotel like the Heerengracht is more convenient. This is a large, modern hotel with twenty or more stories and three restaurants. The roof restaurant where you would dine on your first night has a magnificent view of Table Mountain and it is worth taking the elevator a little early to see the lights come on, transforming the scene to a glowing wonderland as the lights spread up towards the mountain like stars in a darkening sky.

From Cape Town you will want to explore the Cape Province but I suggest you spend your first day seeing the sights close to your hotel. The famous flower market is only a stroll away, and the Assembly Buildings, for which a pass is necessary, a little further. I did this and included in my tour one of the finest Churches in Cape Town, the Dutch Reformed Church. A magnificently austere building that reminded me that the fashionable agnosticism of the west finds no echo in South Africa. This was confirmed later when I noticed, motoring on a Sunday, that every little Church in the country had a great concourse of motor cars around it. Going to Church was still, happily, part of the South African way of life.

Perhaps the same day you can make the Table Mountain trip. The cable car that does the last climb to the summit gives one that special experience as if one was swinging into eternity, but the view on arrival is stupendous. Here is sheer grandeur, a view fit for an Emperor. If you are not entranced with cable cars you can nevertheless have a delightful drive along the mountain road and back. The view from this road, though not quite so breathtaking, is grand enough. Table Mountain gave me a feeling of great exhilaration. I thought it was a place I would always remember.

You need never be dull in Cape Town. Apart from the cinemas, there are four fine theatres and the Cape Town Symphony Orchestra performs at least once a week in the City Hall. You certainly must see the Castle, again but a short car or taxi drive from your hotel, for this historic old building treasures much of Cape Town's long history. The Botanical Gardens, to which you can walk in a quarter of an hour, are a sheer delight. If you are a gardener you can treat yourself to an experience here. South African gardening looks so easy and the results achieved are superb. Then one remembers that if you have no cold, no

30

fog and enough rain with one of the worlds highest sunshine records added to a naturally fertile soil, you are starting with a big advantage. You will now be catching the spirit of Cape Town which is an urbane, unhurried spirit with time for conversation and a firm insistance that the computer is the slave not the master of man.

A very pleasant drive from Cape Town, and an expedition that can easily be confined to a morning or afternoon, is a visit to Groot Constantia. This is about twenty miles from the city through some attractive country. The building is really a large Dutch homestead in the 17th century Cape Dutch style. I found it captivating. The antique furniture was quite lovely and the atmosphere, as well as the furniture and the house and outbuildings, has been preserved so that it took no great imagination to picture life as it was led two hundred years ago by the Dutch settlers. The building itself seems to speak of and suggest all the Dutch characteristics and virtues. It is magnificently built and great care and craftsmanship have gone into the work. There is an air of piety about the building and one can easily envisage drawn blinds on the sabbath and a study of the great brass clasped bible that still rests by itself on a small rosewood table. Moreover the building, though comfortable and obviously durable, is not luxurious. This was the home of God-fearing men who worked, married-once – had children and entered their births and weddings and deaths in that great Bible that was their light in the darkness. They believed. They had no doubts. I do not think it was fanciful to read all this into the farmstead of Groot Constantia. I felt I knew a little more about South Africa – and about the South Africans – when I had wandered at leisure through this wonderfully preserved old building.

While staying in Cape Town I felt I must make the

pilgrimage to Stellenbosch, the great South African University which has a world-wide reputation for the standards of its academic curricula and the distinction of its staff. It is a short motor drive from Cape Town to the exquisite little tree-shaded town that nurtures but does not dominate the University.

For those who have academic memories, Stellenbosch is a joy to visit. I had long conversations with a history don, a professor of anthropology, and one of the students training to become a doctor. I also conversed with some embryo lawyers. The talk, divorced for the main part from current topics of passionate but ephemeral interest, took me back to my Cambridge days. As a son of one great University I salute the University of Stellenbosch, which has maintained its traditions of intellectual integrity as well as keeping pace with a rapidly changing world.

While one is in the University town one must see the old Museum, cared for with what amounts to reverence by an elderly custodian. This fits in exactly with the rest of the town and the University. One has the strongest possible impression that here standards matter and the welcome extended to the tourist such as myself is an elegant tribute to the generosity and good manners of the staff and the students. This visit, though it took but half a day, was one of the highlights of my visit.

I think now that you are settled, at least for a few days, I might suggest some trips you can make from Cape Town by car. Of course these are more fully set out in the official guide books you can buy on the spot, but this book is not a guide book. Its object is to invite you to visit this lovely country of South Africa and so detailed route descriptions are out of place or better left to others. Nevertheless I will tell you of some of the trips I made and enjoyed:

I motored from Cape Town to Clanwilliam, about one

hundred and fifty miles on an excellent highway taking a little over three hours to do the journey. Clanwilliam is almost due North from Cape Town and takes one through a variety of country including mountains and the country known as the Swartland, a rolling grain country. In the Spring the whole area becomes a sea of flowers and it is a magical countryside. We stayed the night in Glanwilliam instead of rushing back to Cape Town and the return drive then becomes a pleasure with plenty of time for diversion if one sees an exciting turning that may lead to a new discovery. As when one is motoring in France for example, leaving the national highways which the Tourists are apt to cling to may be very rewarding. You break out of the Tourist world that exists in all countries and join the country of the citizens who live in South Africa and who are often by far the most interesting people to meet. But by now you will be well aware that to me a holiday rushed is no holiday at all.

Obviously you cannot leave Cape Town without doing the Cape Peninsular Drive. It is only forty miles around and one can have luncheon at one of the many secluded and charming little restaurants overlooking the ocean which specialise in fresh fish. Simonstown the great Naval Base, for nearly 150 years a base for the Royal Navy and the main base of the South African Navy, is on your route. The little adjoining town has an old world charm and the Navy and naval tradition permeate the atmosphere. Simons town has real charms. I had lunch at the restaurant at Seaforth which overlooks a delightful beach and felt quite sleepy after drinking half a bottle of a very good Cape white burgundy that was more seductive and stronger than I had expected it to be.

You must certainly see Cape point which is the southernmost point in Africa and from there make your way back by stages to Cape Town. Again, it is of course

33

possible to dash round the Cape Drive in an hour and a half, but if you do it in the way I suggest then twice the enjoyment can be had and one has time to talk, to enquire, to take snapshots (though not of course of the Naval base!) and time too to enjoy a beautifully cooked lunch in the open.

Finally, among all the many expeditions that the guide books offer you I think you must include the Chapmans Peak drive, again about forty miles, if only because it includes the charming little resort and beach of St James and the house or seaside cottage of Cecil Rhodes, in which he died. It has been maintained much as he left it and many of his personal possessions and treasures are still in their accustomed place. This was the last resting place of a truly great man. 'Where there is no vision the people perish.' Cecil Rhodes had that vision, though his white South Africa stretched from Cape Town to Cairo in the communications field. Africa to him was one continent and he did not doubt the unique contribution of the white settlers to the whole of Africa. Today, when every conviction is questioned and when a new and fashionable philosophy has all but ousted the old faith, it is an experience to see Rhodes' cottage where a great leader lived and died.

This drive also includes Groot Constantia but, as we have indicated this unique place already, I leave the Cape Point drive to you to study and with it Chapmans Peak Drive. The two together can give you two enchanting days.

As I have mentioned, every kind of recreation including golf, tennis, swimming and just plain shopping and sightseeing is there for the asking in Cape Town. But I spent one of my days differently. Through the kindness of South African friends I spent a day at the races. I had the advantage of having had racing ponies and horses in the East so I was able to talk racing with the stewards of the meeting at Kenilworth.

The chief event of the day was the weight for age Queens Plate, won by In Full Flight which seemed to me to be an outstanding three year old colt. In Full Flight had that sudden surge of acceleration just at the right moment — the last half furlong — which is the hallmark of a great horse. On this occasion he won 'going away' by what I made three lengths, a distance confirmed by the officials. This was a real race. Two other horses, Sentinel and Chichester, looked dangerous at one time, but Champion jockey Raymond Rhodes was able to ride out In Full Flight with hands and knees. It was a magnificent sight, made more pleasing by a winning bet.

One small point delighted me at this event. I found that South African apprentices are issued with a 'feather whip.' This can be flourished, but it cannot hurt the horse, so the young jockeys learn to ride without relying on the dubious advantage of the whip which can spoil a two-year-old for good. In addition I went right through the excellent accommodation for Asians, Coloureds and Bantu. 'They are great supporters' I was told 'we have to provide them with first class accommodation.'

I hope I have indicated enough to attract you to Cape Town. It is a gem among cities, combining progress with tradition in what to me is a perfect combination. I met many tourists. They were genuinely captivated by the Cape, Southern, Eastern and Western and many had lingered much longer than they had intended, the ultimate compliment in tourist terms.

5

A Stop-over at Kimberley

Everyone has heard the story of little Erasmus Jacobs who, in 1866, brought his mother a 'bright pebble' which she gave to Schalk Van Niekerk who sold it as a diamond for about five hundred pounds. It was a twenty-one carat stone of fine quality, but the world only began to take notice when Van Niekerk bought a much larger and finer stone from an African for a herd of sheep and some oxen. It was an 83 carat diamond of unbelievable beauty and was, later, given the name of the Star of South Africa. He sold it for just over eleven thousand pounds but, of course, it was worth a fortune. Now, suddenly, diamonds and South Africa were linked in the world news. This was yet another El dorado. If one was lucky and early one might become rich overnight. And everyone it seems, except a few philosophers, wants to become rich overnight. The fabulous diamond rush had started and it grew like mushrooms after rain. It brought to Kimberley and the surrounding countryside some of the most colourful and ruthless characters who have ever swashbuckled and fought for the stupendous prizes that were there for the swift and the strong. This was before the great organisation of de Beers came into being. The De Beer brothers, who sold their farm and devoted themselves to the exploration and organisation of the diamond business, started in the seventies, that is just a hundred years ago and created in the end the organisation that today virtually controls the mining, grading, and selling of the world's best diamonds.

Among the more decorous characters who gravitated to Colesberg Kopje was a young man of eighteen, the son of an English country vicar. His name: Cecil John Rhodes. He had to the full the sense of adventure, the determination to win success (and riches), the confidence in his own star and the resolution to follow his own judgment and flair that was not untypical of young Englishmen at this period. Young Rhodes had no desire to hug the comforts of parochial life at home. He sought adventure in South Africa and Rhodesia, in full measure, he got it. The real relish of the period was provided by characters like Barney Barnato and the whole era is preserved in the charming and modern town of Kimberley, as well as the Big Hole and the raw diamond mines in the adjacent countryside. So, your weeks stay in Cape Town ended, if you can bring yourself to leave, will you follow the route I took and double back to Johannesburg staying a night or two in Kimberley en route? Then we can go down to Durban and explore Natal and visit one or two of the great game reserves before we end our South African holiday. This is not the most economical tour of South Africa. Obviously, if you look at the map, one would preferably visit the same places but in one continuous sweep starting at Johannesburg – and Pretoria – then going to Durban and Natal, so by the flower route to Cape Town. One would then explore the Cape and finally return to Johannesburg by way of Kimberley. The visits to the South African game reserves would then be part of one's Natal stay, but I am following for you my own route because it enables me to give you, I hope, a clearer picture. I do not have to write of attractions which I did not see myself. Following my own itinerary I can vouch for what I describe and then you can adjust your schedule to suit your purse and your inclinations.

It is of course understood that on all these routes the fine service of internal networks maintained by South African Airways takes you swiftly by comfortable jet planes from one place to another, in this case from Jan Smuts to Kimberley and from Kimberley to Johannesburg.

Some tourists miss out Kimberley because 'they have not got time.' It is to my mind a great mistake. This town speaks eloquently both of the pioneering past and of the determined furture of South Africa. Out of a wild scramble and considerable chaos, one of the world's most important industrial adventures has been forged. And it all depends on the unique attraction of a shining, pure white (in most cases) stone, that reflects the light and gives it back with lustre in a rainbow display of red, blue and orange. There is no stone like it. It has created legends around the world. It is every woman's desire and has taken its place, along with mink, as the most luxurious equipment of beautiful women. For me to miss out Kimberley was impossible. So, with real sorrow, I left the Cape. I could have lingered there for weeks, perhaps for life, but I made myself board the plane that in just over one hour would land me at Kimberley Airport. Then I booked in at the Savoy Hotel, Kimberley.

The Savoy Hotel, Kimberley was one of my favourite hostleries in South Africa. It was not grand or luxurious, but it was very comfortable and the service was splendid. It had a pleasantly colonial air of serenity and composure. It ran on oiled wheels. I slept early that night and awoke suitably early next day to explore the town and the diamond scene including the Big Hole. The breakfast menu was in English and Afrikaans and by comparing the two versions I learnt my first words of Afrikaans. Good morning! was Goeie Môre! Grilled fillet of Scotch kipper was Gebraaide Skotse Haring; and Hot scones were Warm Botterbroodjoes ... You will notice that at the Savoy Hotel, kimberley there is none of that continental breakfast myth. When we eat, we eat ... I eat with relish.

Only with breakfast finished and my incidental lesson in Afrikaans completed, was I ready to explore Kimberley and all that the name Kimberley implies. I was well rewarded. Kimberley is fascinating. Apart from the Big Hole where it all started, the authorities have taken the trouble to preserve the old Victorian Kimberley as it was in the early days. Then Barney Barnato was having trials of strength with the Joels, young Mr Rhodes was deciding that he would be a millionaire before he was thirty and the de Beers, the cleverest business organisers and entreprenuers in this somewhat wild initial pioneer period, were laying, carefully and with much acumen, their plans for what these days we should call — with our passion for latin words — the rationalisation of the diamond industry. No doubt the de Beers thought of it as merely founding their empire on sound lines and attempting to assure its future. This was of course long before Sir Ernest Oppenheimer arrived in 1902 to organise the South-West Africa Consolidated Diamond Mines.

One of the biggest of the early finds was made by pure accident. A group of diggers were playing poker in the evening near Colesberg Kopje. A native servant returned home drunk and was told to go out and look for diamonds to make him sober up. He returned within a couple of hours with a fistful of diamonds. The poker session ended abruptly. The employer Fleetwood Rawstorne was the winner of this particular prize. We do not know if the drunken servant, Damon got a reward. Maybe he did and drank away his winnings. Kimberley now was ceasing to be a tent town and a collection of wooden shacks. It was becoming a town and was organised as such, though it bore little resemblance at this time to the neat, modern, and well kept South African City it is today.

With over three thousand very small claims and primitive methods of extraction, the industry was in chaos and it was this that brought in the men with brains, whose watchword was consolidation.

A terrific business battle developed between Barney Barnato, the immigrant son of an East End of London Jewish shopkeeper and Cecil Rhodes, the son of the Church of England and his partner Mr C.D. Rudd. No two men could be more unlike than Barnato and Rhodes but each was as tough and determined as men could be at this period. A battle royal then went on for years but in the end Rhodes, backed by the Bankers Rothschilds, won and Cecil Rhodes became Chairman of De Beers Consolidated and arney Barnato a 'Life Governor', whatever that meant. What it did mean was that Cecil Rhodes was the undisputed boss of this amalgamation. Rhodes did not win for nothing. He had to pay out over five million pounds sterling to the Kimberley Central Company for their assets.

During the war of 1900 De Beers played a great role in defending the town against the encircling 'Boers'. It was beseiged for four months but then this British outpost was relieved and the seige was raised. Kimberley, one way or another, was always in the news.

It was not until 1929 that Sir Ernest Oppenheimer became Chairman of De Beers and from that date the modern diamond industry dates. De Beers has now had Mr Harry Oppenheimer as Chairman from 1957 and he has expanded and diversified this unique industry, with industrial diamond grit being produced in South Africa, Ireland

40

Cape Town Centre (*Photograph by Satour*)

Overleaf—Vineyards at Franschoek, Cape Province (*Photograph by Satour*)

Elephant herd, Kruger National Park (*Photograph by Satour*)

Overleaf—Lions in Kruger National Park (*Photograph by Satour*)

and Sweden. He firmly supports the close organisation of the diamond industry in its production, distribution and selling and answers a question often asked by the public: Is not the diamond price artificial. Should not diamonds be a lot cheaper. He points out that when the crash came in the thirties and the supply of diamonds was reduced because demand had almost vanished, the syndicate held vast stocks and had to abide by contracts that assumed a fairly even development. The diamond industry as we know it today almost went under but it fought its way out of a terrible situation. In order to prevent any such future disaster the present tight control is essential and, as he points out, it benefits everyone — De Beers, distributors, salesmen, those members of the public who hold valuable stones and ultimately the small buyer who knows that when he or she buys a diamond carefully they have an increasing asset in their possession. Not least to benefit are of course the diamond workers, whose future is guaranteed by the system.

When I was in Kimberley I asked some questions about the contract labour system that is also from time to time attacked. The contracts are for a year or nine months and are a popular form of employment because the wages are good and the amenities much better than are usually obtainable. I think the criticism is mainly inspired by ignorance and is directed against the fact that during their contract these men are not permitted to leave the stations where they reside. There are, of course, amenities for sport, libraries, cinema etc, and on compassionate grounds a man may be allowed to visit say a sick wife during his contract. The answer is that this kind of security is essential to the very special business of mining diamonds. Fluctuation in the work force and the consequent difficulty of identifying workers would be disasterous. A diamond is very small — and very valuable. For every considerable diamond mined, tons of waste are discarded. As carried on today under the guidance of Mr Harry Oppenheimer, the industry is a modern one and within the security needs that are part of the very nature of the industry, the worker has a good life. Incidentally those who do not know the Bantu speak of the agonies of separation when the man of the family is absent for a year. This is simply not the Bantu philosophy. Just as in the past the warriers used to return to their women folk after long wars, triumphant, and this was a welcome pattern of life, so the mine worker having saved a large proportion of his wages — because virtually everything is provided free — housing, food, drink, working clothes, recreation — returns home to his wife and family. It is the current vindication of his manhood. Bantu men prefer as a rule to work away from their families. There is still a strong feeling that, when they are at home, apart from an annual ploughing, the women should do the work. This old and strongly held conception of the married relationship is not perhaps as strong as it was but it is still the basis of the relationship. Unless one knows this it is not possible to understand how content the mine worker is with his lot.

Before we leave Kimberley we must take a good look at the Big Hole where the original mine was sunk. It is now filled with water of a peculiar green stillness. It is a vast cavern and birds fly over the water, the only life to stir in this haunted reminder of a mine that yielded hundreds of tons of diamonds in its day. Looking down on it from the adjacent platform, it seemed to me to speak a silent tribute to the immense energy and determination that had carried this industry forward from very small beginnings of an accidental and fortuitous type to its present world-wide success. The Big Hole is the testimony of years of endeavour and eventual triumph.

Before you leave Kimberley you will be taken to the

office where replicas of great diamonds can be purchased. To any woman these are great fun and exciting in themselves. Made from a substance mined near Kimberley they are beautifully cut and at night they sparkle and glow . . . When worn without explanation at a party the effect can sometimes be electric.

So we pay our reasonable bill at the Savoy Hotel and catch our South African Airways plane for Johannesburg, the great city. I was sorry to leave. In Johannesburg, men are grappling with modern business, aided by the new techniques, by a mine of data, by the very reliable computer, but here in Kimberley it all started with the hands of men breaking down the earth and scratching for the elusive bright stone that might make them rich. No doubt diamond mining is more like other great enterprises, but it will never be the same, for this industry depends, to an extent no other does, on the sagacity, the boldness and the intimate knowledge of their trade that the diamond men have. I do not apologise for staying two days in Kimberley, because I believe its story will fascinate more and more tourists – and both the husband and the wife will fall under its spell. There is time yet for the lights of the great city, for the wide golden beaches of Natal and Durban and for the Safari camps where we shall meet the lion, the giraffe, the hippopotamus and the gazelle. We must not miss that plane . . .

6

"*Joburg*"

As the reader may have noticed, I am partial to South African Airways. And not without reason. Apart from the magnificence of their international 'jumbo' routes, their internal services in Southern Africa are, I think, a model of what such services should be. Having experienced the comfort, the careful safety precautions – often skipped by other airlines on short flights – the excellent service and the punctuality of S.A.A. domestic flights it was no surprise to me that my flight to Johannesburg from Kimberley arrived on time to the minute nor that the service for getting one through the airport into one's car was fast and efficient. Porters are always available in South Africa and I found the white air crews, including the stewards and stewardesses, did their job as if they enjoyed it. The passenger was very much the important person and one did not have that uncomfortable experience that I have met from time to time that both the air crew and the service crew only wanted to be rid of one so that they could return to their own lives as quickly as possible. I think that when you have travelled on South African

Airways, either on their inter-continental services or on their domestic and African flights, you will share my opinion of them. Certainly if you ever have any complaint it is taken up immediately — and acted upon.

So here we are gliding into Jan Smuts again but this time taking a car ride back to Johannesburg for a stay. Of course the choice of hotel accommodation here is very wide but for me it was the President Hotel. I plead guilty to having had for years a preference for the rambling, old fashioned hotel with gardens, slightly inefficient and altogether human, but I must admit that the President, a great block rising up into the Johannesburg sky, was a very comfortable place to rest in. The bedroom had every conceivable comfort, the variety of dining rooms — from snack bars to elaborate french orientated 'cuisine' — meant that you could get exactly what you wanted to eat when you wanted it. All the ancillary services were efficient and quick, including the laundry. The native staff who attended to the bedrooms were controlled by immediate white management and the premier dining-room was of course complete with its maître and its headwaiter. I discovered that I was as comfortable in the President as I had been anywhere in the world. I could not find a writing room, a library or a billiard-room but the old conception that a grand hotel should try to duplicate life in an English or American country house or in a French chalet or a German Castle or indeed in a Venetian Palace, has long been disbanded. Hotels like the President are the Hotels of the seventies. All one needs to add to that is that the President manages to convey the impression of personal care of its patrons, and an efficient public relations office instantly smoothes out any difficulty in the unlikely event of such an occurrence. Salute then to the President Hotel, the best of its kind. Johannesburg has its critics. I am not among them. They say it is a monster dedicated to the relentless pursuit of wealth and with no standards other than a money standard. I did not find it so. After visiting the British publisher William Collins, represented in the city by William Collins South Africa, I spent several days exploring the magnificent shopping centre round Eloff Street, visiting a gold mine and watching the delicate intricacies of diamond cutting. I found it fascinating.

The whole vast city hums with activity and industry. Everyone is going somewhere – fast. I found it a bracing tonic after the warm seduction of the Cape. Here we are six thousand feet above sea level and the climate in all seasons is invigorating, the summer heat being abated by the great height. I was told that I should find the altitude trying at first. I never noticed it beyond feeling exceptionally fit, active and energetic. I began going places – fast, like the other citizens of this great city. Before I made any excursions I visited local places of interest that were near at hand, in my case, the Witwatersrand University, Milner Park, the Union and Leydon Observatories which are situated on Hospital ridge and the Herman Eckstein Park which contains a Zoo. Again I had not previously liked Zoos very much, but here the animals seemed to me to be cared for with real consideration of their special needs. I found driving around Johannesburg exhilerating and I found the citizens, if one could persuade them to slow down, human and often clever and remarkably kind and well informed.

South African Railways and many important firms, both South African and foreign, have their headquarters in Johannesburg. This makes it a great international and cosmopolitan city. Europeans outnumber the Bantu population and a big Bantu township adjoins the city. I visited this and found the houses with their electric light and main water and the garden land that surrounded the house quite different from the kind of conditions that are so often made the subject of documentaries in Europe and America. I found this intensely interesting though I realise that the average tourist would not have time for such visits. These can take a whole day if one converses, as I did, with the local witch-doctors and the modern herbalists, some of whom have grown rich and whose medicinal recipes have a startling record of success — perhaps due to the fact that their patients have more faith in them then we have in the potions of our highly trained doctors.

Every tourist in Johannesburg should, however, visit a gold mine. It is much easier to visit a modern gold mine or indeed a platinum mine than it is a diamond mine. The mining of diamonds is, as we have seen, of necessity wrapped around with a security blanket. Gold and platinum, though very valuable, are not so easily concealed and if one applies in advance one can arrange mine visits very easily. It is worth while. These great gold mining operations are the industry on which Johannesburg sprang to life and greatness. When the early Afrikaans settlers left the Cape to cross the Vaal river and live a free life under their own leaders, it was with agriculture in mind, new pastures for their cattle, fresh grazing grounds for their oxon. But the discovery of gold added a new dimension to the life of the Transvaal and was the one event that made the North rich. As I write this, the price of gold today has reached an all time high and one can be sure that it is a story of boom conditions in the Transvaal, very welcome after some difficult years.

It was the discovery of the large Witersrand mine in the eighties that started South Africa as one of the Worlds chief gold producers, but it has been the deliberate stabilising policies of the industry that have secured for the Republic a gold industry much less upset by rises and falls in world markets than the gold industries of other countries.

I do not have to stress that the city of Johannesburg, which has tendrils of trade and commerce around the world, provides its visitors with every kind of entertainment excluding the pornography and polluted films one now sees in the West. It is a happy, bustling, extrovert place and from it one can make expeditions to many interesting places in the Transvaal. I was fortunate enough to have two English friends, who had retired, in the Honeywell district and we spent several happy days at their beautiful cottage on over six acres of land laid out as garden and fruit paddock. They were looked after by an African who had been in their service many years, with his wife and — if I remember correctly — six children. It was a very happy home and the relationship of the owners to the family who served them was one of great understanding and helpfulness. They were concerned in the lives of their family in a way one no longer sees in Europe or America.

On those sunlit days we played croquet on their lawn, drank South African wine for lunch and, I must confess, in the evening were somewhat reluctant to return to Johannesburg. But return we did and then the city reasserted its magic and we were swept back into its busy life.

From Johannesburg, it goes without saying, one must visit the administrative capital of South Africa by making the journey along an excellent motor route about forty-five miles to the north. Pretoria was named after the Boer hero Andries Pretorius and indeed all this Transvaal country is imbued with the Afrikaans spirit, though many of the largest firms are controlled by English speaking directorates. The distinction is becoming daily less evident and perhaps less important as a definitely South African personality rapidly emerges to take over from the previous historic divisions of the country. However, Johannesburg is still the heart and soul of the nationalist Party and a visit to the State capital is necessary to complete for the intelligent tourist his picture of South Africa.

Pretoria also has its critics, who say it is stuffy and bound by red tape, but I can only say I found this an illusion. I enjoyed the comparative quiet and dignity of its straight streets and boulevards and shaded walks and parks. I stayed in Pretoria three nights and was not bored. I found the civil servants, both at the top level and in the lower grades, intelligent, remarkably progressive and extremely well informed.

Apart from the usual attractions you will find in your local guide book, there is a charming old British fort and strongpoint that remains preserved on a hill just outside the city. It is a fascinating place. I found the capability of the authorities to care for and preserve with equal understanding and attention all the memorable places that played a prominent part in South African life a pleasing trait. It has certainly added enormously to the enjoyment of the present day tourist who is constantly able to see, revitalised and in its original condition, many places that had they not been protected and restored would by now have vanished either through the forays of the builder or from the creeping envelopment of nature itself.

As you are staying in Johannesburg for a few days you will wish to explore the places of interest within fairly easy reach and I now mention some of them, though this really is guide book territory and you should supplement my suggestions (arising out of my own necessarily limited experience) from the much more comprehensive list the official guide book will give you.

If you feel like escaping from the busy embrace of Johannesburg, there are smaller and some of them typical towns of the Transvaal within easy reach. Among others are: Springs, Brakpan, Benoni, Boksburg, Germiston, Roodepoort and Krugersdorp.

One should know that the Rand is a series of valleys running for fifty miles on the Transvaal high veld. This country was formerly regarded as barren land but the discovery of gold has made it the centre of intense industrial activity. Mines, with their white dumps, are scattered along the gold bearing reefs. One is motoring in a world of gold. This is not tourist country but for those visitors whose business compels them to centre their activities on Johannesburg it is good to know that there are drives outside the city. Perhaps it is worth mentioning that during the warm summers, nearly all the rain, about 30 inches a year, falls often in the form of thunderstorms. I have already mentioned that these are on a gargantuan scale when they occur, as if the gods themselves were weeping. A splendid chorus of vibrant thunder and lightning accompanies the downpour that often goes as quickly as it comes.

Johannes Rissik, after whom Johannesburg was named, was the Surveyor-General of the Transvaal and the town was originally laid out to accommodate the ox-wagon outspans. Now it has to cope with an immense traffic including buses and taxis. The taxis are segregated but you will probably not notice this. The taxis with white drivers gravitate naturally to white fares. It is not easy for the visitor on his first arrival to understand how easily and smoothly separation works in practice and those who have spent several weeks in the Republic often say that they have noticed no signs of any system to separate the races.

As we are in Johannesburg and money is the business of this great city — it has without doubt the most modern banks anywhere in the world — I should mention that the currency is the Rand, equivalent to about eleven shillings in English currency and one dollar thirty cents in American currency. The Rand is divided on the decimal system so this presents no problems. If you have stayed in

Johannesburg, then almost certainly it is business that has accounted for your stay. In return we may say that the business visitor will find every comfort and convenience imaginable to carry on his work in Johannesburg.

If your business is finished, or if you have arrived in South Africa with no business but pleasure in mind, you will almost certainly include our next port of call on your itinerary. Durban, on the Indean Ocean, is a playground for very many South Africans as well as visitors and rightly so. From Durban we can take a plane to the great Kruger Game Reserve, without equal in either Europe or America, or for that matter in Africa.

Although Johannesburg is business orientated I was sorry to leave. I found that the activities of the city were so diverse, the people so lively and well informed, and the whole vibrating life of the city so compulsive that I missed it after I had left. Here was not the mellow charm and tradition of London or Vienna or the brittle brilliance of Paris, but instead here was a city made in a matter of decades by men who accepted gladly the challenge of a material age, as if to say: 'Well if these are the rules of the game, we can play it as hard as anyone . . . '

There is a sturdy spirit of adventure and independence in the Transvaal, coming no doubt from the first South Africa Republic, which after the Sand River Convention of 1852, had its headquarters in Pretoria and Johannesburg.

I almost forget to mention that throughout the country there are numerous hot springs and warm springs that have healthy and curative properties. I took the trouble to seek them out and my health, already made robust by the clean invigorating air of the high veld, became even more rude. The springs have not really yet been commercialised and they are delightful and unique. By the way, the water as well as the wine is excellent in South Africa, and they make perhaps the world's best coffee. They even make tea.

The newspaper you receive with your morning tea, if it is the Rand Daily Mail, almost certainly contains strong criticism of the Government. This will make you feel you are back in Europe or the States. It is a strange magic in South Africa that makes each tourist feel a visitor or guest rather than a foreigner. It is a tribute to a generous and open people.

But now we head for the delights of Durban and intend to stay longer than before so that we may get to know Natal which has an atmosphere and a way of life of its own, perhaps because of its large English speaking population which includes a very numerous Indian colony. South African Airways again waft us on the route to Durban. We glide down into a moist green land, very lush and find a warm and hospitable people.

7

Durban and Natal

I have so far followed the plan of telling you only of places which I visited myself and were on the route I took throughout the Republic which I think has certain advantages because the reader may sense that the narrative is not taken from travel brochures, from books, or from the literature of the firms in the Tourist trade, however good these may be. Naturally such books, booklets and brochures tend to follow a uniformity of presentation, style and treatment and the reader becomes aware that many of them are based on what others have written before. Nevertheless there was this disadvantage in my method: like all other visitors, although I spent far longer than the average tourist holiday in the country on two separate visits, I was not able personally to cover the whole field. There were places and areas of great interest which I simply had not time to visit and in order to include at least some of these I had to decide how to present these unvisited places. Should I continue the narrative in which case the reader might assume I had been there, or should I tell the reader and describe these places from information I had gathered? I decided to tell the reader, so that now in the plane on the way to Durban from Johannesburg it seems a good time to mention two places of great interest which I have omitted from the story so far because I did not visit them personally or merely visited them briefly.

When I visited Stellenbosch University I became so interested in the University itself, its academic activities and in the whole University life that I did not travel through what is known as the Stellenbosch wine route. This is a district to the west of Belleville which you can easily visit from Cape Town. The whole rich, mild countryside is filled with wine farms or vineyards. The homsteads of the growers are often old and beautiful. You could, if you were a real devotee of wine, spend several days touring this magnificent wine country. Each farm has its special and favourite wine, for instance, Green land produces fine sherries and dry red wine of a superior quality. Verdun owned by a Mr Roux (a South African name) specialises in dry red and white wine. The Spier Estate has a title deed dating back to 1692 and produces a great variety of wines and mantains some lovely buildings as well as the modern pressing equipment and storage areas.

The grapes used by most of these South African wine growers are world famous names like Steen, Hernitage and Tinta das Borroccas and Pinotage.

The roots of the South African wine business, if one goes back far enough, have their origin in the traditional wine culture of France, Germany and Spain, but the Cape wine industry has now been so long established that South African wines are of a quality that compares favourably with a European vintage. Years ago South African wines bottled and labelled their wines more or less along the traditional wines of Europe. But now the time has come for more and more independence in presentation, for the fact is that South African wines represent a new chapter in the world wide business. Greatly superior to American or Australian and equal to European wine, they are often cheaper than wine of a similar quality in Europe. I sometimes think that South Africans when selling their wines abroad do not take a confident enough view of the merits of their wines, some of which are superb. So confident and energetic in most walks of business this is not characteristic of them and I would like to see a more aggressive attack on foreign markets and a more ingenious use of the various media to make Cape wine the table wine of the world. I hope this suggestion will not be taken amiss, but I was so impressed with the quality of Cape Wine which in fact 'travels' very well that I felt sure that Cape Wine had not got its rightful share of the market. Even Jugoslavian wines, not distinguished for the highest quality, but quite good, had often won markets that South African wines in my opinion could have won.

The South Africans, of course, wise people, drink a lot of their best wines themselves, but with increasing production I hope that the export markets will be greatly enlarged. The Cape Wine Farmers Association may be interested in new possibilities. Meanwhile the Stellenbosch Wine route should not be missed by the tourist. If it converts him or her to South African wines instead of the 'plonk' which is now invading the European and American market, it will have done both the wine industry and the tourist a favour, for South African wine has great purity and is a delight to drink with meals.

I mentioned briefly the hot water Spas of the Transvaal but had not the time to visit them all. The baths which are curative and entirely a natural phenomenon are still largely undeveloped. However very comfortable camps have been made on the sites and it would be a complete change on a South African holiday to visit some or at least one of the spas. There are a large number of baths to choose from but Warmbaths is the nearest to Pretoria. It is in the course of great development, but my advice is to go and visit these places now while they are still simple and comparatively inexpensive. Facilities are already available for cures for the large range of ailments and conditions that respond to hydrotherapeutic treatment. For instance there is an excellent hospital at Warmbaths as well as camping and caravan sites. For the more adventurous there are more remote warm springs. The countryside abounds with them and there is no doubt that this aspect of South African Tourism will play a much larger part than at present in the years to come.

I mention here the wine and the warm water springs again in order to give a fuller indication of what the Tourist who has the time should see. I can imagine no more novel and delightful way of spending a couple of weeks than in a leisurely pilgrimage through the Cape wine country – tasting as one progresses – and exploring the warm springs of the Transvaal which would take one into country off the beaten tourist track . . .

But while making notes on this small diversion, our air trip from Johannesburg to Durban is already over and we are being greeted by friends at Durban airport. Having settled into our hotel, on the following day we start to explore Durban and Natal, this important province of the Republic. There is much to see and much to charm the visitor.

As soon as one arrives in Durban one becomes aware that Durban is a unique town in South Africa. Commercially it has a world renowned harbour and port. Climatically it is warmer and moister than the Transvaal and is the favoured resort and playground of South Africans themselves. The Hotels along the seafront are big and handsome and the whole town has an air of dignity and

South African Airways Boeing 707 over SA open spaces
(*Photograph by South African Railways*)

Swaziland, Swazi matron (*Photograph by Satour*)

Cable car and climber on Table Mountain, Cape Town

tranquility. The province of Natal, of which Pieter-maritzburg is the capital, has an unusual border. The independent States of Swaziland (well worth a visit) and Lesotho, as well as the Transvaal and the Cape to the South, are its neighbours and it is a very old settlement. To the North is Zululand destined to become the independent state of Kwa-Zulu. Natal has neighbours of great variety and this perhaps affects the character and habits of her population.

I was struck by two aspects of Durban. The first was the lovely greeness and semi-tropical flowers and vegetation and the corresponding delight of the winter climate and also the climate of Spring and autumn – though quite a number of tourists prefer the summer heat. The second impression was the large numbers of the thriving Indian community descended from 19th century workers imported for the sugar plantations. The presence of the Indians gives Durban a cosmopolitan flavour that one does not meet with elsewhere in the Republic. The growth over the years of the Indian community to a position of affluence and importance is a tribute to their own industry and to the progressive policies of the South African Government who have incorporated this very large community into the life of South Africa.

It was Vasco de Gama of course who first landed near where the city of Durban now stands and a delightful memorial to him decorates the town. The memorial is gay and even garish but altogether pleasing. An adventurous piece of work to recall a great adventurer.

The Dutch had a trading post at Durban but abandoned it and in 1823 Lieutenant Farewell of the Royal Navy started an English settlement that eventually lead to Natal becoming an English colony. It is now of course an important part of the Republic but its history, including the wars with the great Zulu King, Chaka, left their mark and the Natal we see today is the child of all these adventures and long historical associations.

From the extremely comfortable hotels on the water front one overlooks the mile long Marine Parade. This is made into a paradise for children – and their parents – with every kind of diversion and aquatic diversion including mini pleasures boats that are self propelled. The unusual aspect of what amounts in fact to a pleasure ground, is that it has been contrived without vulgarity or untidiness. No blowing papers, no dark and dirty corners, no vulgar advertising. It is a model of what such places should be. And it makes Durban a wonderful resort for the man with a family. It is the best attempt that I have seen anywhere to provide pleasure and recreation for children in perfect safety, only a few steps away from where they may be staying with their parents.

In Durban there are sights to see both historic and modern and the most efficient local tourist office will provide you with a guide book that will tell you all you need to know. However, may I mention a really fine library that delighted me by listing twenty-eight of my books – other authors are represented fortunately – and a museum which I found fascinating. This was a triumph for the museum because I can get bored in a museum as quickly as I can in the theatre, an unpardonable trait.

You will not want to spend all your time in the city of Durban though one could well do so with pleasure. I made several trips from the city, one to Pietermaritzburg where I saw several top European jockeys, including the world famous Lester Piggott, competing in a special international race. I made one, too, to the valley of a thousand hills which is rightly a Tourist attraction because one has this panorama of valley after valley stretching away to the horizon as if a giant had made great ravines one after the other until he was tired. No one who has seen this strange and beautiful piece of South Africa ever forgets it.

I was lucky enough to be asked to one or two of the very fine houses outside Durban. These are as imposing and as beautiful as anything that America or Europe can show and the warm climate aleviated by the fact that the country rises some fifteen hundred feet quite near Durban — itself at sea level — enables the wealthy owners of these properties to have gardens ablaze with frangapani, roses, bougainvilia and many other beautiful shrubs and flowers. They are getting the best of both worlds, the mild, moist temperate climate and the semi-tropical. It is enough to make many European gardeners green with envy.

I also motored south along the coast road and called in at Isipingo Beach, a very popular place. But what struck me and fascinated me was the number of beaches that had not been developed, just golden sheaths of sand with nothing more than a track leading from the excellent road to the sea. More and more of these lovely and often deserted beaches are bound to attract the developer in the years ahead, though the South African Government keep an eye on the adventures of private enterprise, being well aware that the countryside, unspoiled, is a major tourist attraction.

I have made the point before but it has so much relevance that I repeat: Visit South Africa while there is so much of its natural beauty remaining. Fortunately with the creation of great game reserves and with a consistant preservation policy the South African countryside is in no danger from the vandals who have spoiled so much of Europe and in particular the south coast of France, until quite recently beautiful and now much desecrated.

We should really devote a chapter to the story of Durban Harbour, one of the great harbours of the world and now more than a century old. Its rapidly expanding business has been made possible by constant new improvements and increased capacity. The sugar terminals themselves are a model of modern efficiency. Durban is by far the largest Port in Africa and its business has been increased even more by the closure of the Suez Canal. It is worth a visit.

So this is Durban, but I confess I cannot wait to take you on safari. For it is from Durban that one will make the short air trip to the great Game Reserves that are the pride and wonder of South Africa. Will you come with me then and see at very close quarters the lion, the zebra, the hippo, the elephant, the buffaloes and all the antelopes that abound in these reserves? You will be entering another dominion, not that of man but that of the animals. I recall when I first had that experience in South-East Asia. It is quite uncany. The message comes through strong and clear. You are now in our country. Take care.' So it was in South Africa. And so, I hope, it will always be.

8

The Great Game Reserves

South Africa is so rich in great game reserves that no Tourist can hope to see them all. The largest, for instance, is the Etosha Game Reserve in South-West Africa which is twenty-six thousand square miles in extent – as large as some small countries. The most famous of all is the Kruger National Park which runs to nineteen thousand kilometres – eight thousand square miles – and abounds in lion, elephant, hippopotamus, wildebeest, zebra and giraffe. This is the mecca for many Tourists and a number of reliable tourist companies run air services to the excellent accommodation. At Kruger the greatest care is taken of the visitors and the land-rovers and buses have strong windows and are wholly enclosed – and air conditioned.

Contrary to rumour, which would have it that the animals are so used to being photographed and inspected that they have become tame, the herds are completely wild and dangerous if one does not know what to do and what not to do. At Kruger the safari guides are most expert and are able to tell their parties how to behave when, for

61

instance, approaching lions. I spent one day at Kruger when I should have spent a week or at least three days, but on my return visit I made up for this by flying by Comair to the Rand airstrip of MalaMala which is accurately described as being the luxury Game Reserve of South Africa. Luxury in this context means charming african style bungalows with bedrooms and private bathrooms, excellent food and all the comforts.

However, wild animals are just that and the MalaMala reserve of 50,000 acres of untamed bush veld has a fine array of lions, rhino, hippo, zebra and giraffe. The camp of MalaMala itself is in remote and very beautiful country and one can spend some days there that pass very quickly. The routine is to make two forays a day after game. In the evening a carcase of meat is left for the lions and the guests go out in an open land rover and take refuge in a wired compound from which they can watch the lions when, eventually they appear, hesitatingly at first, then with growing confidence. It is a truly fantastic and awesome sight, the great beasts tearing the meat apart, the strong eating first and then the young and the old . . .

When they have finished, one by one, they will walk quietly away and then there is fifteen minutes of deadly silence. But out under the cover of the veld the hyenas are watching. They are making sure that every lion has departed, quite, quite sure. Then there is a stirring and swiftly, silently the hyenas lope in to gather the scraps which the lions have left behind. It is a parable in behaviour and one speculates whether our restraints on the rule of the strong are really anything more than frail and fashionable.

One morning I persuaded a ranger to take us with him on a very early morning safari. This is another experience again. One is apt to see much more game and in bigger numbers in the early morning, before or just after dawn. It is a rewarding experience and when at last one gets back one is hungrier than one had thought was possible . . .

MalaMala really has everything. The filtered swimming pool is a delight. The service is impeccable and the magnificent 'lounge' decorated with great heads of the animals is a good place for conversation. There is even an air conditioned bar, but all this sophistication has not been allowed to spoil the essential business of MalaMala which is to show its patrons wild life as it really is. MalaMala is one of the few reserves where entirely open landrovers are used, but in fact the security is tight. The ranger drives and has a loaded and very heavy revolver within reach. An African sits on a raised seat behind the car carrying a game gun in case of emergencies, so that in the unlikely event of a crisis very quick action can be taken. On occasion the four or five passengers have to cooperate. For instance on one occasion we met the lion herd before we reached the hide out and before they were expected. They sat there on rocks just above us and at the edge of the path along which we had to travel to reach the rendezvous. We stopped dead and the ranger asked us not to move. Any sudden movement of an arm or a hand may frighten lions and make them aggressive. I think it is fair to say we sat frozen in our seats. Then, when the lions had become accustomed to us, very gently the engine was started and at an even pace and quietly we slipped through the pride. None of us had been so near to lions in their wild state before. I shall not forget it.

A point that is often missed is that men spend a fortune on uncomfortable safaris with·the ambition of 'bagging' the lion. Personally the thought of killing even one of these great animals appals me. They can be photographed and even that takes some nerve and ability. And compared with a hunting safari, MalaMala is inexpensive and in my opinion just as good — or better.

I think that it adds enormously to the interest of the Game reserves if one knows something of the background of the animals that roam there. The rangers will tell you of their habits and way of life, the indications that they are passive, or afraid, or disturbed, their eating habits and the best times of the day and night to observe them. But there is more to it than this and I have made out for you my own brief note on each of the great wild animals you will see through your binoculars or even when very near to you without them. This includes some indication of their history because their past, as well as their present, is fascinating.

ELEPHANT

There are two species of this immense mammal, that which has its habitat in India and South-East Asia; and the African elephant far wilder and apparently more difficult to tame, more dangerous when roused and perhaps for this reason more worth pursuing.

In spite of its traditional wildness the African elephant was trained centuries ago. Hannibal took two hundred fighting elephants with him on his crusades of conquest. The Carthaginians had three hundred war and service elephants in Carthage alone, Hasdrubal numbered one hundred and forty elephants in his campaigns against the Romans, and Caesar showed elephants to the multitude in the arena at Rome . . . In the East, of course, the elephant was the sure insignia of Kings especially the 'white' elephant and it seems that early Roman Emperors and their foes had much the same view of the elephant. He was the badge of strength and power, a part of the Army, a wing of the establishment, shedding more lustre on the leader.

Knowing this strange history, perhaps you will look with even more interest at the Elephants in South Africa which are ferox naturae. This is a noble beast with a regal tradition.

Elephants have a very limited sense of sight but an acute sense of smell. One approaches them against the prevailing wind, preferably choosing a position much higher than where the elephant is grazing. Then, in the unlikely event of the elephant being 'disturbed', one has plenty of time to vanish. I think the sight of a fine herd of elephants is one of the great natural sights of the world. After many years knowing about elephants and even riding them in Asia, I am still thrilled by the sight. So when you see it, look well. It is an unforgettable experience.

RHINOCEROS

I must confess that the Rhinoceros fills me with alarm. I know this is irrational and that protected by a good and very expert ranger (as well as by the African perched on his high seat with his gun at the ready) I am, so to speak, as safe as houses, but perhaps the fact that I do not feel that way accounts for the peculiar fascination of this great primaeval animal now found in large numbers in the game parks and reservations of South Africa.

The rhinoceros, in the beginning, roamed the world over but is now confined to Africa south of the Sahara and to South-East Asia. His domain is much smaller than it was but it is still considerable. The square-lipped rhino, at one time in danger of extinction, is now multiplying fairly rapidly. In another book I would like to tell the great success story of the South African game reserves and the part they have played in the conservation of wild life, big and small.

I think my own healthy fear of the Rhino derives from the impression I have that he is anti-social. I do not think he very much likes man and I feel that his instincts are not really curbed by any notable process of reasoning. In other words, if he feels like charging, he charges. Of course in practice this does not happen. Your ranger knows exactly how and where to approach a herd in order to avoid incidents. Still a charging rhino must be a fearsome sight. They can move much more rapidly than their vast unwieldly bodies would give you to suppose and the reflection that their eyesight is poor and they cannot turn with agility I find only moderately consoling.

The black rhino is about eleven feet long and five feet in height. The 'square-lipped' Rhino is the largest rhino in Africa. It measures over twelve feet in length and about five and a half feet to the shoulder. The Rhino, often at one time called Burchell's Rhino, is found South of the Zambesi. Its nature is said to be more urbane than the black rhino and those who have eaten rhino meat say it is excellent. Because of its limited location we may regard the square-lipped Rhino as the treasure of Southern Africa and of South Africa in particular.

THE GIRAFFE

I love Giraffes. They are the gentlemen of the animal kingdom. Gentle and mild in disposition, if attacked they will face their enemy, even lions, and defend themselves vigorously. They are gregarious, moving in small troops usually in open ground. The make smashing photographs because the tallest reach up to eighteen feet, a spectacular sight.

Giraffes also have a history. The Emperor of Germany in 1215 was sent one as a present from the Prince of

Damascus. Julius Caesar, a confirmed animal – and slave – collector had some on display in Rome, part of the bread and circuses routine. The 'Soldan' of Egypt sent one to Lorence de Medici who was of course Grand Duke of Tusacany; and Mohamed Ali, the founder of the last Egyptian dynasty, presented one to George IVth. Unfortunately it found Windsor Great Park cold and died. The Giraffe it is clear was a favourite royal gift. It was after all a little unusual and that was what the donors were looking for.

This ruminant feeds on mimosa and any other succulent plant and its enormously elongated neck and long, tough tongue aid it in its search for such food.

Giraffes are often very obliging and will stand stock still if you are quick enough to photograph them. But the next moment with a swinging lope they are off, retiring in good order away from human curiosity.

LIONS

The lion really earns his title of King of the jungle and like all monarchs should be approached with considerable circumspection, with care but without fear, observing as it were the protocol, the rules of the game which your ranger will explain to you.

There are several breeds of lion, but the 'Cape Lion' which you will meet in South Africa was formerly divided into those that were predominantly yellow and those that were brown. There is now said to be no real distinction except that of colouring, which in any case changes with age. Lion cubs are mildly striped but grow out of these markings. Lions are lazy, very good to their cubs, ferocious only when hungry. Occasionally an old lion whom the pride has rejected will turn man-eater. Livingstone was

contemptuous of the lion's roar, an arrogance I do not share.
I find it the most terrifying noise given out by any live
creature.

Lions of course have always been regarded from biblical
times as a sign of strength, and at least one African
Monarch, the Emperor of Ethopia, has the popular title of
the Lion of Judah. He keeps lions as pets and as a symbol.
I have never visited Ethiopia, but I recall with pleasure that
when the Emperor lost his country for a time and was
exiled in London, the Cambridge Union Society made him
an Honorary Life Member, a reward I was fortunate
enough to achieve myself.

All in all, a pride of Lions is a sight you will always
remember and one still is slightly relieved when the thrill is
over . . .

ZEBRA

Here again we have, as it were, a South African specialty.
The Zebra roams often in fairly large herds and can be
difficult to photograph as it is sensitive to the presence of
man and swift to escape his attentions. The background
colour is white with regular stripes. A special breed is
found north of the Orange river. This has different
markings and is perhaps even more beautiful. The zebra
has from time to time been crossed with both the horse
and the ass, though not with very happy results. Zebras if
attacked defend themselves in a body, instinctively adopt-
ing the national motto ex unitate vires. Their chief defence
is a devastating kick that can kill.

The Zebra of South Africa is one of the most attractive
of all the wild animals and if you can get a good, clear
close-up photograph of a herd you have been clever,
patient and lucky.

BUFFALO

Those who are acquainted only with the domesticated working buffalo of Asia can have little conception of the magnificence and power of the wild 'Cape' buffalo, often measuring over nine feet and weighing as much as two tons. This magnificent creature was known as the Cape Ox, the Buffel, and the Bokolokolo, used by the Bechuanas. The horns are massive, very broad at the base and tapering, making a deadly weapon. Buffalos which will not attack unless wounded sometimes have a battle royal with lions. The lion does not always win and there seems to have been some kind of undeclared truce between the two animals.

Buffalo graze and wander in herds, sometimes quite large ones. Again they are difficult ot photograph. It is a mistake to approach too near. I myself was content to copy an excellent photograph I was given, but you may be more adventurous and wish to obtain your own snapshot. I wish you luck.

I hope that these short notes on some of the most famous wild animals in South Africa may be of interest to you when you go on safari. In any case you will enjoy safari life. It is the great escape everyone is looking for.

9

Some special resorts

South Africa has so many small resorts, some of them off the main highways, that no visitor and very few South Africans have visited them all. However, I have checked in each case the official descriptions of these places, many of them staggeringly beautiful and well worth visiting if you can fit them into your itinerary. In each case I have added my own comment and the reader may be assured that the resort or place of interest in question is accurately described. If you are motoring through South Africa between flights, you will be able to reach many of these beauty spots either on your route or by a small diversion. Sometimes the visitor who is willing on occasion to turn off the highway is very well rewarded. I have chosen a dozen such resorts from the parts of the country where visiting tourists are most likely to roam. In several instances the place itself is in reality more beguiling than its description, unusual in tourist literature.

WILLOWMORE

Willowmore is situated about 200 miles from George on the National Road between Johannesburg and Mossel Bay. This town has a hotel with 35 rooms, a hospital and a number of garages with a breakdown service.

Visitors are urged to pay a special visit to the historic farmstead of Schilpadbeen, approximately 15 miles from the town.

The road through the Baviaans Kloof is renowned for its beautiful scenery. Mountain zebra, the Willowmore Cedar – which attains a height of 130 feet and a diameter of almost 6½ feet – as well as Bushman paintings are all to be seen along this route.

The Beervlei Dam is situated approximately 19 miles from Willowmore on the Aberdeen road and is a well-known water ski-ing resort.

ABERDEEN

The Dutch Reformed Church at Aberdeen – built in 1910 – is known for its tower, which is the highest church steeple in the country and leans slightly to the right.

In Aberdeen there is much of interest to the visitor. A visit to Fonteinbos, on the banks of the Kraai River, where fossilised footprints are to be seen and where the visitor can relax on the site complete with barbeque and other facilities, is definitely worthwhile. The Caravan Park is centrally situated, and conveniently close to the shops andFormal accommodation can be obtained at the hotel. Rooms with private bathrooms are available and the cuisine is first-rate.

BEAUFORT WEST

Beaufort West, centrally situated in the heart of the Great Karoo, provides easy access to the picturesque Meisingspoort, the Swartberg Pass, the Cango Caves and the Ostrich farms of Oudtshoorn. Beyond is the famous Garden Route with its sunshine and beautiful beaches.

Tourist attractions in the town itself are the interesting collection of antiques in the new Library building and the Old Town Hall, which has been proclaimed an historical monument.

Beaufort West has a dry, invigorating climate which makes for pleasant winter vacations in particular.

Provision is made for campers at the modern caravan park in Donkin Street on the Cape Town side of the town. Here, baths, showers and waterborne sewerage have been supplied for the convenience of visitors; the tariffs are extremely reasonable.

A golf course, tennis courts, bowling greens, a recreation club, the municipal swimming baths, centrally situated parks and children's playgrounds ensure the holiday maker of a pleasant stay in this Karoo town.

For those who like angling, the Gamka Dam in the Nuweveld Mountains, about 10 miles to the north of Beaufort West, provides pleasant hours in the open air. Permits for visiting the dam or for angling are obtainable at the municipal offices.

Beaufort West and vicinity is renowned for its breathtaking display of wild flowers in the spring; at this time of year, particularly along the national road between the town and the Swartberg, visitors can take delight in the vast variety of wild flowers.

Again, conveniently on a National Route.

LADISMITH

Ladismith lies at the foot of the Kleinzwartbergen, with the majestic Towerkop in the background. It is a peaceful, shady town with a friendly atmosphere in which the traveller in the Little Karoo immediately feels at home.

Hoeko, a few miles from the town, with its vineyards and orchards along the mountain slopes and in the valleys, puts the visitor strongly in mind of the Rhineland. This is the birthplace of C J Langenhoven, the Afrikaans author, poet and creator of 'Die Stem'. The house in which Langenhoven was born is still to be seen in this picturesque valley.

The at-times rugged Karoo landscape, relieved by the charm of heavily-wooded mountain slopes where nature has been tamed, presents the traveller with an unforgettable and interesting experience.

Sevenweekspoort is especially renowned for its scenery and colourful rock formations. The road winds between ravines and crags and crosses and re-crosses the clear mountain stream, in which one may see the rare Aristata Protea, in addition to the great variety of plant life. The traveller can stay over in these picturesque surroundings at the Aristata Caravan Park where the tariff is very reasonable indeed.

Anysberg, paradise for succulent collectors, Prins River Poort and Dwars River, picturesque valley where top quality fruit is grown and the Garcia Pass with its natural flora, where the Erica Heath flourishes, are only a few places which are within easy reach of the visitor to Ladismith.

Two first-rate hotels provide pleasant accommodation, while campers can stay over in pleasant surroundings at the caravan park situated to the north of the town.

For the mountaineer, Towerkop and the Kleinzwart-

73

bergen present a challenge where he can pit his strength against nature on the rough rockfaces and crags.

BARRYDALE

This picturesque little town is situated on the main road through the Little Karoo. The fertile Tradouw Valley, the scenic Tradouw Pass, the Warmwatersberg, the Karoo region and the Brak River, with the Bellair Dam on the North and the Anna Roux Wildflower Garden just outside the town, are worth a visit.

The visitor to Barrydale will definitely find a trip to the famous hot springs at the Eastern tip of the Warmwatersberg a rewarding experience.

Accommodation is provided at the Warmwatersberg Baths with its guest house with indoor baths, and on the eastward side of the town in the Anna Roux Caravan Park, which has every modern convenience.

Visitors I have met say that Barrydale is an oasis of peace.

CALITZDORP

Calitzdorp is one of the small, tranquil towns of the Little Karoo and is known for its sunshine and dry, invigorating winter climate.

Beautiful scenery, particularly the strange red koppies adjoining the national road to Prince Albert through Buffels-Kloof and Kruis River, welcomes the visitor to this region.

Accommodation is available in the hotel in the town itself, or, for those who prefer outdoor living, there is a pleasant camping site on the banks of the Hwis River along

74

the national road between Calitzdorp and Ladismith. Every facility the camper may need is available. There is no charge for the use of the site.

The Hot Springs on the banks of the Olifants River, approximately 15 miles from Calitzdorp, are being re-planned and laid out at a cost of several thousand Rand. The complex is being planned to straddle both banks of the Olifants River with the hot springs at its centre. The complex will consist of swimming baths, a restaurant and a safe swimming pool for toddlers. Only the best and most modern cloakrooms and amenities are being provided, and for those who prefer a little solitude there are private bathing cubicles, equipped with a bath and a bed, where visitors may enjoy the salutary effects of the mineral waters undisturbed. Sauna bath facilities are also being introduced to enhance the luxury of the holiday resort.

A large caravan park and tourist camp with special modern ablution facilities are also being laid out.

A part of the holiday resort is going to be made available as residential plots to private owners who will be able to erect their own holiday home or permanent residence there.

The holiday resort on the Olifants River promises to be an ideal stopping-over place for all nature lovers who want to pay a visit to the Mountain Zebra Park or who are on their way to the North, or are returning.

Calitzdorp will become a very popular resort.

GEORGE

George is favourably situated in a picturesque environment on the coastal plateau between the range of the Outeniqua Mountains and the Indian Ocean. It is easily accessible by road, rail and air. The planning of a large modern aerodrome has reached an advanced stage.

George is the second Drosdy to be established (in 1811) and is named after the then reigning monarch, George III. The natural beauty of the country-side – indigenous forests, magnificent mountain ranges (George and Cradock Peaks are 4,379 and 5,224 feet high respectively), deep valleys with dark ·water flows and the lakes complex – is widely known and attracts thousands of visitors yearly.

Glentana, Herolds Bay, Victoria Bay, Wilderness and Swartvlei are seaside resorts situated within a range of from 6 to 15 miles from George. Geographically, George is the centre of the Garden Route and these seaside resorts and other places of interest are consequently within easy reach. The so-called 'Lakes Road' winds between the Wilderness lagoon, the upper Langvlei, the lower Langvlei, the Rondevlei and the Swartvlei lagoon and gives, inter alia, an impression of the wild bird life abounding in this region and the beautiful indigenous bush-covered country -side.

Apart from making use of the modern Outeniqua Pass, visitors can also use the Montagu Pass, which was completed in 1847. The old Voortrekker route is clearly marked and visible and can be seen from the Outeniqua Pass.

A modern Municipal Tourist and Caravan Park is provided, and because of the uniform climate of George (average summer and winter temperatures of 22.8°C and 20°C 75°f and 71°f respectively) it is a point from which thousands of tourists visit the coastal resorts, the lakes, the forests, etc. as well as the Karoo hinterland.

KNYSNA

Seldom has nature endowed a region so lavishly with its

beauty as it has done in Knysna.

As of old, Knysna is today still the resting place for the weary traveller, a haven for those seeking peace and tranquility, a pleasure resort for the holiday maker, a paradise for anglers, sports enthusiasts, and nature lovers. Knysna has something and more for everyone — excellent residential areas; unexcelled scenic beauty; rocky coasts and calm inland lakes; sports fields in picturesque surroundings; shady camping sites and caravan parks; an unsurpassable climate; a wealth of its indigenous forests.

From Knysna the following splendid daily excursions are available:

> Goukamma Nature Reserve and Buffalo Bay (12 miles).
>
> Upper Lagoon, Old Road and Phanton Pass (19 miles).
>
> To Belvedere, Brenton Estate, Brenton on Sea (19 miles).
>
> Main Forest, King Edward's Tree, the Glen, Buffel's Neck, Paardekop, View Site, Wittedrift, Keurbooms River, Plettenberg Bay, Garden of Eden, Bracken Hill Falls (67 miles).
>
> Belvedere, the Lakes, Wilderness, George, Barrington, Rheenendal, Phantom Pass (76 miles).

Moderate weather conditions prevail throughout the year; the gentle rains fall for the most part at night and during the day the holiday maker can enjoy hours of pleasant sunshine.

Knysna is the perfect combination of mountains, forest, lake and sea.

The words 'a paradise for anglers' is almost an understatement.

PLETTENBERG BAY

Plettenberg Bay is situated just beyond Knysna on the road to Port Elizabeth.

There are three beaches with safe bathing for those who like swimming.

Deep sea anglers come from all over the country to the famous fishing spots of Plettenberg Bay where yellow-tail, garrick, red steenbras, tunny and stumpnose abound.

The Marina on the Keurbooms River has moorings for more than a hundred craft, and is a popular angling and skiing resort.

A golf course, tennis courts and bowling greens ensure a pleasant vacation for the sports enthusiast.

A number of caravan parks, two first-class hotels and furnished flats, which can be rented from local agents ensure a pleasant stay.

For the busy executive, Plettenberg Bay has a daily air service operating between Cape Town and Port Elizabeth.

I visited the bay. It is lovely.

SEDGEFIELD

Sedgefield is a peaceful little coastal town on the mouth of the Swart River, approximately 19 miles from Knysna. Situated as it is amongst the lakes, holiday bungalows and caravan parks, in picturesque surroundings and excellent angling spots, Sedgefield is a small paradise to which every year thousands of visitors return. The great variety of indigenous bird life found in the vicinity of this coastal town draws enthusiasts even from abroad to study the movements and habits of the bird life in the idyllic atmosphere of the lagoons and lakes.

SOME SPECIAL RESORTS

MOSSEL BAY

Mossel Bay, rich in places of historic interest, is the home of the milkwood tree, generally accepted as the first 'post office' in South Africa, because of a Portuguese seaman who, in 1500, secreted a letter in an old shoe which he hung up in the tree. This tree (centuries old) overlooks the bay where the first European set foot in Southern Africa almost 500 years ago, and still serves as a post office today. The letters are posted in a post-box shaped like a Portuguese mariner's shoe, after being specially stamped. The area around the tree has been laid out by the Municipality. Also to be seen here is the Da Gama Padrao (stone cross), a gift from the Portuguese government.

Mossel Bay is the most important coastal town between Cape Town and Port Elizabeth, with a busy harbour and business community. Owing to its refreshing climate, sparkling blue sea and white beaches it has, quite justifiably, been described as the 'Naples of South Africa'. Mossel Bay offers much of interest to the tourist. The Harry Giddey Park, with its great variety of indigenous plants and shrubs and even a small game reserve, is situated within the town and includes well cared-for bowling greens, a playground for children and tennis courts. Even a quiet walk through the park will relax and refresh the tired traveller.

The Shell Museum contains more than 700 varieties of South African shells as well as a large collection from all over the world, and does justice to the rare and colourful shells which are found along the Southern Cape coastal line with its warm ocean current.

The Historical Museum in Church Street houses some remarkable antiques, including a cast of the famous Mossel Bay stone, which was discovered in 1850. In the Voortrekker Museum, Hartenbos, there is a wide variety of antiques to be seen, many of which were collected during the symbolic Ox-wagon Trek in 1938.

The Bat's Cave, below the lighthouse on the Point, with its historic relics, casts the modern traveller's mind back to the days when the coasts were still inhabited by Strand-lopers. An interesting phenomenon is the large number of bats that hang suspended from the roof and walls of the cave during the day.

There are ample recreational facilities for the holiday maker: Modern golf course with a marvellous view of the sea from every hole. Tennis courts and bowling greens in Harry Giddey Park.

Excellent facilities and club house for yachtsmen at Munro Bay.

Mossel Bay and its environs is a paradise for deep-sea and rock anglers. Here all kinds of fish await the angler – the big ones as well, like the Black Marlin of 301 lbs caught by Jackie Wheeler in 1957 and which now graces the walls of the Poort Restaurant.

First class accommodation is to be found at the four hotels and three motels serving the area.

All accommodation is under the personal supervision of people with years of experience in the hotel and tourist industry, which serves as a guarantee of full satisfaction for all holiday makers and tourists.

The white beaches of Mossel Bay are renowned through-out the country for their safety.

Santos Beach, the bathers' paradise, the Bakke, popular venue for campers and surfers and Hartenbos, with its impeccable huts, rondavels and caravan park, draw thousands of holiday makers from all over the country every year.

The Poort provides a safe tidal pool, fashioned by Nature itself, with a bottom of shimmering white sand.

At Diaz Beach provision is also made for the Coloured

community where holidaymakers may lease plots and build their own holiday cottages.

I stopped long enough in Mossel Bay to admire the breathtaking beauty of the white beaches.

RIVERSDALE

Riversdale, situated in scenic surroundings beneath the Sleeping Beauty mountain peak in the Langeberg range, is the home of a rich variety of wild flowers and the famous Erica Blenna, which in its natural state grows only on the slopes of the Sleeping Beauty.

Jurisch Park, at the entrance to the town from the national road, is well-known for its beauty as a wild flower garden. Riversdale is rich in the heritage of bygone days.

The Julius Gordon Africana collection, which is being preserved on display in the Versfeld House, includes valuable furniture, paintings (among others a number of Bowler and Volschenk originals) and other objets d'art.

The original Zeekoegat Homestead, where Sir Harry Smith spent a night in 1835 on his way from Cape Town to Grahamstown, historical buildings like the original Dutch Reformed Church, the St. Matthews Church and the old Post Office, are only a few of the sights to be enjoyed by both tourist and historian.

For those who appreciate the fine and interesting reminders of a bygone era, a visit to the mouth of the Duivenhoks River, approximately 30 miles from Riversdale, holds great promise. There, at the Puntje, projecting in the azure waters of St. Sebastian Bay, the visitor finds close to the waterfront the peaceful atmosphere-drenched *kapstyl* houses with their thatched roofs and low, white-washed walls.

Riversdale is known to every visitor travelling the

Garden Route for the top quality accommodation which the town's hotels offer the tourist.

Visitors may also stay over in the picturesque and popular municipal tourist camp and caravan park, where every modern convenience is available to make the visitor's stay a pleasant one.

A game and Nature Reserve is being developed just outside the town, in close proximity to the national road where a large variety of flora and fauna can be seen.

ALBERTINIA

Owing to its situation, about halfway between Riversdale and Mossel Bay, people travelling the Garden Route prefer to stay overnight at Albertinia. First rate accommodation – for non-White servants as well – is provided for the traveller at the hotel.

Albertinia is renowned for its heath and proteas. The Erica Bauera is found only in this region, varying in colour from crimson to white.

Again accessible from the national road.

STILL BAY

Sun and sea combine to make the perfect holiday. 8 miles beyond Riversdale en route to Mossel Bay, the tourist turns off in an easterly direction and after travelling a further 19 miles reaches this peaceful holiday resort on the sea, at the mouth of the Kafferskuil River. Every year the beaches of Still Bay – probably the most beautiful and safest in the Southern Cape – draw thousands of holiday-makers from all over. The hotel at Still Bay offers first class accommodation to those who want to enjoy the sun and the sea in peaceful surroundings and is renowned throughout the country for its sea food cuisine and its Africana collection.

The Kafferskuil River enters the sea amidst scenes of natural splendour. For several kilometres upstream the river is perfectly safe for small craft. It is a specially popular venue for those interested in calm water angling and water sport.

Still Bay is a mecca for rock anglers. On the westward side the angler finds picturesque fishing spots among the rough rocky coast and here dreams of hooking a big 'un become reality.

Jongensfontein, 5½ miles north west of Still Bay, is another angling paradise from which the angler seldom returns empty handed.

The harbour provides a haven for the fishing boats which bring ashore almost 300 metric tons of fish every year.

The caravan park, only 150 yards from the beach, has 300 sites, modern conveniences, fireplaces and a restaurant for campers.

Two miles north-east of the beach for Whites, and adjoining the well-known 'Pulpit' is the beach and camping site for Non-Whites, with modern conveniences and fireplaces.

In the spring, Still Bay and the area around becomes a paradise of wildflowers, vygies, lilies and proteas, and is visited regularly by South African flora enthusiasts. Still Bay's mild climate in the winter months affords a pleasant holiday for those who want to enjoy a rest before the rush of summer visitors begins.

Jongensfontein is situated 5½ miles north west of Still Bay and is known in particular for the natural swimming pool among the rocks, which affords a safe bathing spot for children.

So much beach, so few people!

SWELLENDAM

Swellendam boasts of a rich historical heritage. The historic Drostdy was constructed in 1746 and today houses a unique collection of antiques. The Drostdy Museum includes the 'Old Gaol', the Gaoler's House and an open air museum.

Visiting hours are from 8 a.m.-1 p.m. and 2 p.m.-5 p.m. Mondays to Saturdays.

Other historical buildings in the town are the Old Residency, Auld House and the 'Oefenhuis' (an old Slaves' Church).

Swellendam is situated at the foot of the Langeberg range; the town and its environs offer the traveller many interesting sights.

The Bontebok Park is situated about 3 miles out of town and is open to visitors during the following hours: April-September 9 a.m.-6 p.m. October-March 8 a.m.-7 p.m.

There are nine species of game in the park, including Bontebok, Springbok, Eland, Buffalo, Grysbok, as well as about 170 bird species.

The mountain drive takes the visitor through beautiful mountain scenery at the foot of the Langeberg; permission to use the road may be obtained from the Forestry Officer. There is no admission charge.

The Tradouw Pass between Swellendam and Barrydale is renowned for its beautiful scenery and Bushman paintings, about 1500 yards from the road.

Swellendam has three hotels, a well-equipped caravan park in the town and a camping site at the Stroom along the Bree River, about 4 miles out of town.

For the sports enthusiast, facilities for golf, tennis and bowls are available.

HEIDELBERG

Heidelberg is a peaceful little town along the Garden Route between Swellendam and Riversdale and forms the centre of a primarily farming community. About three kilometres from Heidelberg the traveller turns in an easterly direction and arrives, after a further 25 miles, at Witsand and Port Beaufort at the mouth of the Bree River. The rivermouth is navigable for several miles upstream and is a popular angling and seaside resort. However, there are no hotel or camping facilities.

Heidelberg is real farming South Africa.

* * *

Carefree young travellers will probably be quite content to go their own way and drop in on such resorts as these, staying if they like it and moving on when the urge takes them. For those who prefer to know rather more before committing themselves, and especially for those who have a private schedule, in each case the Town Clerk of the resort will provide full information on all the facilities, recreations and accommodation.

The Town Clerks in South Africa are a dedicated body of men and really do seem to love their posts. I found them most helpful and useful.

10

The Summing-up

Although from experience I am firmly of the opinion that flight by South African Airways is by far the most convenient way of getting around in South Africa – the distances involved make too much motoring tiring except for the young – still we must say that the great network of modern roads that link all the great cities make motoring a joy, if one does not press on always wanting to reach a destination that is too far away. I motored the shorter distances in the Republic and found the comparatively uncongested roads with superb surfaces and with magnificent scenery often there for the asking, very exciting. South African motorists seem to be a slightly milder and mellower breed than their European counterparts and no wonder, they have the time and the space. Your International driving licence will see you through and there are no breath tests. Drivers are not expected to drive if they have had a lot to drink. Mr Jorrock's motto 'Where I dines I sleeps' may come in handy. The police, though usually tolerant, act swiftly there in case of accident. Remember that it is as much an offence to injure a small African boy as it is to injure a Government official, but I hope you will avoid doing either. Please remember to have spare oil and petrol. Some of the distances between garages and petrol pumps are long in comparison with the average in Europe and America. But the motoring associations are most helpful and you will really enjoy your motoring in South Africa, a free and delightful experience.

The train services of South Africa are punctual and good and, if you possibly can, take the new Blue Train from Pretoria – Johannesburg – Cape Town to experience real rail travel luxury. This magnificent train is at the moment without equal either in America or Europe.

The schedules of this super train are in the appendix. Roughly speaking you embark in time to dine and arrive after a fairly early breakfast. Do not miss it if you can possibly help it. It is the train of tomorrow, today.

The supremacy of the new Blue Train should not dazzle you into ignoring the other excellent services that South African Railways provide and the schedules of these too I have inserted in the appendix, which is up to date at the time of going to press but can of course by checked in a current train guide. Train travel is restful in South Africa. Service is exceptional.

There is so much information that the Tourist might like to know and in a book of this size one can only indicate it's range. However, the Department of Tourism has all the detailed information for you when you arrive and its officials are really there to help. The slightly stuffy official attitude which visitors to the European continent sometimes complain of seems to be entirely absent in South Africa. They really take an interest in your particular needs and will make out a schedule for you to fit your requirements and inclinations. They are also very good about children, knowing exactly how to cope with a family holiday in the Republic.

I hope you visit Zululand. The Zulus are an upstanding race and their country, now called KwaZulu, is large and varied. I was lucky enough to travel by car on the good dirt roads to see the interior of Zululand and to meet Prince Goodwill, their hereditary chief, who received me with cordiality and kindness. You must see a Zulu troupe of dancers. They are earth shattering! The vibrant energy and pride of the Zulu man comes through in their dances and you will watch spell-bound. Zulu dancers are now said to be coming to Europe to give performances, but see them in their own country, near to the land they love. They are by nature and tradition herdsmen and are a unique people. The University of Zululand is also well worth a visit. A new capital is being built for the new State.

Just one hundred and sixty miles from Durban is Safari Lodge and its Game Reserve. This is another most comfortable place, with the round African-style accommodation and all the most modern conveniences. Although MalaMala is my personal favourite, I have to admit that the Zululand Safari Lodge, for those who demand everything, is very hard to beat. It is unique in having a water hole less than a hundred yards from its dining room and early in the morning or in the evening herds may be seen coming down to drink. This does not imply that they are tame. They have merely become accustomed to this water hole and regard it as 'theirs.' If it was taken away, the game would go too.

The Zululand Safari Lodge has its own airstrip for those who prefer flying to motoring under any circumstances, but for me a three hour drive on a fine motorway from Durban is entirely acceptable and I prefer it to the small plane of a private company. However, many visitors think otherwise and you will make your choice.

The most common fault of tourists in South Africa as

elsewhere is that they are prone to think that they have to make a certain place by a certain date. This ruins any holiday, except for the over-meticulous who are not happy unless abiding strictly by a schedule. The ideal way to proceed is to have an overall plan with plenty of scope for alterations and diversions en route. The pace of life in South Africa, though brisk in some of the big cities, notably in Johannesburg, is not pressurised outside these big towns. Someone once said that happiness consisted in falling in with one's environment. Certainly one misses the flavour and the relish of a South African holiday if one brings New York, or London or even Paris with one. A new country should be savoured and tasted like good wine, not gulped down. The faster one goes, as a rule, the less one sees.

For Sports addicts, South Africa is just what they pray for. Mountaineering, hiking, golf, tennis, caravan expeditions, safaris, all forms of fishing and aquatic sports including surfing, they are there for the asking and the South Africans, sportsmen themselves, are only too willing to show you all the facilities they have. The constant but usually temperate sunshine is of course ideal for all sport and incidentally South Africa is a wonderful place for painters to paint and for writers to gather material for novels of the contemporary scene or for historical works. The great epics of South African history, the struggle between the British and the Dutch, the rising of the Zulus leading to the two Zulu wars, and the multi-racial population of the country from the beginning, make the scene a rich one for the writer and historian.

Nor need you leave your culture behind in Europe, for, as I have pointed out, in Ballet and in Opera South African artists now excel and the South African stage and cinema has its own merits. As for the news, each morning there are any number of newspapers to bring the news to your breakfast table and I found the quality of the journalism high. There is of course, as befits a sophisticated people in an age of change, a great debate going on among South Africans as to what changes will suit their country and can be accepted without endangering law, order and peace upon which the welfare of all South Africans, European and Bantu, depends. If the visitor tries to understand the special position of South Africa and her importance to the free world, I think this is appreciated. We all like to have friends.

One of the features of South African life that pleased me was that there was no television and so one was spared the fashionable banality that has now overtaken so many television stations in Europe and in the United States. Moreover, the lack of television has induced the South Africans to read and they are notably better read than the television-addicted generation. However, this happy state of affairs is coming to an end, for within a year or two the South African authorities are setting up a national television body. Let us hope that it is a patriotic station and takes a proper pride in South Africa. I think that this will be so, for South Africa is not prone to the malaise of denigration and self-abuse which has infested the West. I have no doubt that television, when it comes, will be welcomed by the public, and tourists will feel more at home than ever.

I liked the great Universities of South Africa, as the reader already knows. Any visitor who wishes to see the educational scene would do well to visit a South African University. They are the South Africa of tomorrow and you will hear a lot of good sense talked there.

There are all kinds of commercial and industrial activities of interest to the visiting business man. I visited a famous platinum mine and saw the whole process. Russia is now just the leading producer of platinum but South

Africa is catching up fast and will probably be the world's biggest producer in a very short time.

Firms with offices in South Africa have available to them modern facilities for conferences, mostly but not exclusively in the cities. Business is always on the move in South Africa — new stainless steel plants, extended platinum production, oil exploration in Zululand and on the continental shelf. South Africa, although it has achieved so much in seventy years, is only at the beginning of its vast expansion, on the way to becoming one of the world's rich nations. The need is as much for good type immigrants as for any new technique or project. This future of expansion poses its own problems, political, social and financial but South Africa has the gift of grappling with her problems as they come and those who know the courage and the brains of these people do not doubt that her future will be infinitely more prosperous and progressive than her past.

The story of sugar production in South Africa reveals the spirit that drives this country on. It was in 1852 that Edmund Moorewood found that he could produce sugar easily and well on his farm at Compensation. As so often happens with pioneers, he could not raise the capital to press on with his discovery and emigrated to Brazil. But his efforts had not gone unnoticed and other farmers stepped in to experiment and develop cane sugar and found the great sugar industry of South Africa and Swaziland, centred largely to the north and south of Durban, where the climate is ideal for growing.

It is this kind of drive and refusal to capitulate when adversity comes their way that accounts, I think, for the buoyant South African economy and the absolute faith in the future of their country that characterises South Africans, whatever their business or profession may be.

So we have travelled thousands of miles in the Republic.

We have seen the great cities of Johannesburg, Pretoria, Durban and Cape Town. We have seen something of the life of the people and perhaps divined something of their pride and character. And as Tourists we know that this is no ordinary country to visit.

If you decide, as I hope you will, on a South African holiday you will never regret it, for you will see many things you cannot see elsewhere. You will remember the blue haze over the mountains and the lush valleys of Natal, the quiet charm of the Cape and the throbbing activity of Johannesburg. And I think you may well remember what it is that all good vacations or business trips alike depend on for success — the generous welcome of your hosts that will make you want to return to this enchanting country . . .

Appendix

1. *Weather statistics — Sunshine hours in South Africa in comparison with other cities* (average per year):
   London-1,480 hrs; Paris-1,740 hrs; Rome-2,360 hrs; Washington-2,200 hrs; Honolulu-2,400 hrs; Los Angeles -2,600 hrs; Canberra-2,628 hrs; Madeira and the Canary Islands-2,650 hrs; French and Italian Rivieras-2,700 hrs; Cape Town-2,980 hrs; Johannesburg-3,150 hrs; Pretoria -3,240 hrs.
2. *A list of all the Tourist Information Offices in the RSA*
   The Department of Tourism, 28th Floor, Poynton's Centre, 124 Church Street West, Pretoria.
   The Director, Cape Peninsula Publicity Association, P.O. Box 863, Cape Town.
   The Secretary, Oudtshoorn Visitors Bureau, Municipal Building, Church Street, Oudtshoorn.
   The Director, East London Publicity Association, P.O.

Box 533, East London.
The Director, Port Elizabeth Publicity Association, P.O.
Box 357, Port Elizabeth.
The Director of Publicity, P.O. Box 628, Kimberley.
The Director, Publicity Association, P.O. Box 4580,
Johannesburg.
The Director, Publicity Association, P.O. Box 925,
Pretoria.
The Publicity Officer, P.O. Box 288, Bloemfontein.
The Director, Durban Publicity Association, P.O. Box
1044, Durban.

3. *A note on the Blue Train*
The Blue Train is a luxury, air-conditioned train serving
Pretoria, Johannesburg and Cape Town twice a week.
Accommodation is available with private facilities in the
compartment. Travelling time is approximately 24
hours. A single ticket, Johannesburg to Cape Town, is
from £44.02.

4. *The Visa and Customs Regulations*
Visitors who need passports but no visas:
Citizens of the United Kingdom and Dependent Ter-
ritories. Canada, Malawi, Mauritius, Rhodesia and the
Republic of Ireland, who are of pure European descent.
Nationals of Portugal who are permanently resident in
Mozambique. Nationals of Switzerland and Lichten-
stein.
Visitors who need passports with visas:
Nationals of all countries not mentioned above. All
persons not of pure European descent, regardless of the
country in which they are permanently resident. Persons
without nationality or of undetermined nationality.

Customs
Visitors may import, duty free, new or used goods to
the combined value of R50. This includes the following
commodities, but no more than the quantities

93

indicated: Spirits, including liqueurs and cordials: 750 ml, opened or unopened; bottled wines: 750 ml; perfumed spirits and toilet waters: 300 ml; cigarettes: 400; cigars: 50; tobaccos: 260 g; All other articles are dutiable except motor vehicles covered by a triptyque or carnet.

5. *Hotel grading in general terms*
   South African hotels are graded according to the International one to five star system. Two and three star hotels are considered tourist hotels and four and five star are luxury hotels.

6. *Tours to the Game Parks*
   There are eleven touring companies which offer regular tours to the Game Reserves from Johannesburg and Durban.

7. *Car hire facilities*
   Several Car Hire companies in South Africa enable tourists to pick up a car in one centre and leave it in another. Very few companies offer unlimited mileage. An International Driving Permit is required when the Licence does not show a photograph of the holder.

8. *Good Tourist maps*
   Tourist maps can be obtained from tourist centres in all major towns as well as some petrol stations in the Republic.

9. *South African Airways Africa's Biggest Airline, a Tourist attraction*
   Since its formation in 1935, SAA has become the biggest airline in Africa, and one of the world's leading carriers. SAA has nearly 70 offices in 25 countries. Currently it operates to 45 points on five continents – Africa, Australasia, Europe, North America, South America. It will soon add a sixth continent to its network – Asia. Services start shortly between Johannesburg, the Seychelles and Hong Kong.
   SAA has pioneered many new developments over the

years. It became the first airline outside the USA to operate the Douglas DC7B at the time the fastest piston-engined aircraft in the world; first outside the UK to operate the world's first pure-jet passenger aircraft; first to operate a regular non-stop service between South Africa and Europe (in 1962); first to equip aircraft with Single Side Band radio equipment, pioneered by SAA and subsequently adopted by airlines the world over; first to introduce the 747B with the new, powerful JT9D-7W engines; first to introduce vanity rooms especially for the ladies; the most modern passenger seating on the UK-South Africa route; and the first to introduce non-stop services between London and Johannesburg, the fastest service on the route.

Between Europe and South Africa, SAA currently operates 16 regular return services a week from 12 capitals. There are services across the South Atlantic to the Americas, and eastwards to the Indian Ocean islands and Australia. From Johannesburg SAA links 10 neighbouring countries and serves 16 destinations within South Africa.

Within South Africa, South African Airways provides a comprehensive network of all-jet internal air services, with the world's most advanced passenger jet fleet diminishing distances between main centres to a matter of minutes. SAA have the prestigious Boeing family of jets at work throughout their domestic network — with certain types also operating on their regional and international route system: 747B, 707, 737, 727 and 727QC aircraft are in service, plus the new Hawker-Siddeley 748 jet-prop which is used on certain regional services.

The Johannesburg-Durban flight is said to be the world's shortest jumbo jet service — and SAA's 747B superjets cover the 312-mile hop in 50 minutes. Johannesburg to East London is about 1¼ hr. by SAA; Johannesburg to

Port Elizabeth is 1½ hr.; Johannesburg to Kimberley is around 50 mins. And SAA covers the 956 land miles between Johannesburg and Cape Town in about 1¾ hr. Services are not only fast, they are conveniently frequent to suit the most demanding business or tourist visitor. At a recent count, for example, we noted SAA operates no less than 110 services every week between Johannesburg and Cape Town and vice versa. Around 48 services a week on the Johannesburg-East London route; 54 services Johannesburg-Port Elizabeth; 38 Johannesburg-Bloemfontein; 37 Johannesburg-Kimberley and vice-versa; 130 Johannesburg-Durban; 52 between Durban and Cape Town; plus a host of flights to intermediate cities and other centres. This regularity of service ensures a large number of seats are available.

SAA's £7m. fully automated passenger reservations and message switching system links its UK offices in London, Birmingham, Glasgow and Manchester with Johannesburg and services world-wide.

At Johannesburg's Jan Smuts airport, the £12m. 747 terminal is a dramatic combination of elegant design and efficiency. Passenger reception procedures at principal airports throughout South Africa are noticeable for simple, efficient passenger handling procedures, with a computerised system which automatically checks in passengers.